IMPROVE YOUR MEMORY
IN 8 SIMPLE STEPS

IMPROVE YOUR MEMORY
IN 8 SIMPLE
STEPS

Nicola Chalton

RIGHT WAY

Constable & Robinson Ltd
3 The Lanchesters
162 Fulham Palace Road
London W6 9ER
www.right-way.co.uk
www.constablerobinson.com

Published by Right Way, an imprint of Constable & Robinson, 2009

A copy of the British Library Cataloguing in Publication Data
is available from the British Library

ISBN: 978-0-7160-2218-3

Illustrations: Pascal Thivillon
Design: Basement Press, London
www.basementpress.com

Printed and bound in the EU

1 3 5 7 9 10 8 6 4 2

CONTENTS

INTRODUCTION

What is memory?

Memory is a process of the brain that involves taking in, storing and retrieving information. Without memory, we could learn nothing. We would merely react to what we were currently perceiving. There could be no art and no culture: no one would remember long enough to produce or appreciate such things. There could be no personal relationships: we wouldn't remember who anyone was.

Memory may involve shared memories of events, like the shared memory of 9/11 or the credit crunch. It can also be intensely personal. Each one of us has unique memories of the people, places, events, smells and tastes we experience every day. These memories of our lives form the threads that connect who we are from childhood to adulthood: our very identities depend on memory.

Because memory is so important it is not surprising that we fear losing our memories, or wish for better ones. Fortunately, there are things we can do to keep them functioning, even to make them more efficient.

An average brain has an amazing capacity to store information: it is said that a human brain can store more

information than the world's most advanced supercomputers
(Baron, 1989). Most of us will never use this vast capacity, but
there are a few people with exceptional memories. They fall
into two categories: those who use special memory techniques (known as mnemonics) to aid recall and those gifted
people who have a natural ability to remember phenomenal
amounts of information (Valentine & Wilding, 1994). How
exactly the born geniuses perform their memory feats is still
not understood, but the memory masters who use mnemonic techniques are exemplified by a remarkable Russian man,
Shereshevskii. The Russian neuro-psychologist, A.R. Luria,
studied his methods and describes the case of Shereshevskii
in his book, *The Mind of a Mnemonist*. Shereshevskii had an
unusual ability to use visual images and associations to
remember things – from hundreds of digits and complex
mathematical formulae to pages of poetry in foreign languages – and to remember those things perfectly years later.
Though we may never have the rare abilities of
Shereshevskii, the techniques he used can be learned.

Do you have a poor memory?

Human beings are not machines and they do not have perfect memories. An occasional lapse – forgetting where you
put the keys, a birthday, a name – is perfectly normal even
for people with so-called good memories. This is because we
are usually adept at remembering some things and not others.
For example, we may be very good at remembering facts but

hopeless when it comes to names and knowing where things are.

Many people believe they have a poor memory and there is nothing they can do about it. In fact, what they have is an untrained memory. Memory training can transform a 'poor' memory into a super-efficient one, and bring remarkable benefits to personal and business life. Techniques for improving memory – some of which were pioneered by the great orators, the ancient Greeks and Romans – can be used to recall anything from a pin number to a vital presentation.

The purpose of this book

This book is aimed at the majority of people who could use more of their amazing capacity to store information if they trained their memories. It is based on the following ideas:

→ No one has a perfect memory and everyone can do something to improve their memory.

→ Most people have strengths and weaknesses in different memory functions. *Memory strengths and weaknesses are assessed in chapter one.*

→ Memory training can increase self-esteem and confidence. For many of us, this is a good reason to want to improve our memories, but the very best motivation comes from specific personal goals, for example, improving memory to help you learn the names of your students if you are a teacher. *Personal memory objectives are identified at the end of chapter one.*

➜ An interest in memory and an understanding of how memory works are helpful if you want to improve your memory. *A background to memory training and the memory process is given in chapters two and three.*

➜ The application of a few simple techniques can make significant improvements to memory, from ways to enhance attention and concentration to specific memory aids for storing and retrieving information. *Techniques for improving memory are covered in chapter four.*

➜ Most importantly, improving memory does not happen without effort. *Tests to practise memory skills are provided in chapters one, five and six. These assess a range of memory types: social / adaptive memory, visual-spatial memory, working memory, factual memory, numerical memory, and verbal and auditory memory.*

➜ Finally, what most people want is not to perform amazing memory recall feats but to make noticeable improvements to their use of memory in everyday life. *This is the aim of the book.*

Note that this book does not provide clinically controlled assessments of memory. Nor is it intended for people with memory loss resulting from disease (dementia) or brain trauma through head injuries. If you suspect that you have disease-related memory loss you should seek the advice of a trained clinical neuropsychologist.

The effort required

There are no short cuts to a good memory. Using memory techniques is a learned skill that requires sustained effort. Start by applying the techniques provided in this book to your normal daily routine. Supplement this by activating your mind: read more widely, learn new things, take up crosswords and other puzzles, solve problems. It will help your memory skills. Develop motivation for improving your memory by working out why you need a better memory. Knowing this will give you a greater chance of success.

1

PRELIMINARY ASSESSMENT

Assessing your untrained memory

This chapter includes a preliminary series of tests and a questionnaire. These are designed to check your memory's current levels of functioning and to identify weaknesses and strengths before you apply memory-improving techniques. Note that memory performance depends on individual interests and experiences and there is no single objective scale against which to measure the effectiveness of your memory. This assessment cannot provide a definitive result but will give an indication of your memory's efficiency, which you can use as a general guide for setting goals for memory improvement.

Before you begin, take a moment to understand the organization of this programme.

How to follow the programme for memory improvement

There are eight steps to the programme featured in this book:

1 Take the tests on the next few pages. Identify areas of weakness in your memory functioning.

2 Keep a diary for several weeks to identify any problems with your memory and the frequency of recurrence. Then complete the questionnaire on page 59.

3 Based on the results of the preliminary tests and questionnaire, list your memory weaknesses on page 63 in order of priority – the first being the problem that causes you most anxiety.

4 Write down the reasons why you want to improve your memory and set your memory objectives on page 64.

5 To put your efforts into context and to understand how memory training works read chapters two and three.

6 Use techniques for improving memory in chapter four to work on your weaknesses, and tests in chapter five to practise those techniques.

7 Take the final assessment in chapter six to check that your memory is improving and you have achieved your goals. This final assessment is more challenging than others in the book. If you have worked through the exercises, and practised thoroughly, your performance should show a marked improvement.

8 Apply the techniques you have learnt to everyday life.

Preliminary assessment

On the following pages there are tests assessing six areas of memory:

Test 1: Social/adaptive memory (names and faces, birthdays and anniversaries, appointments)

Test 2: Visual-spatial memory (scene, abstract drawing, mental rotation, spatial orientation)

Test 3: Working (short-term) memory (playing cards, word pairs, reading)

Test 4: Factual memory (facts, definitions)

Test 5: Numerical memory (mental calculation, telephone numbers)

Test 6: Verbal and auditory memory (word manipulation, word lists)

It is recommended that you complete all the tests. Take the tests when you are in good health and feeling wide awake. Find a quiet place away from distractions. You will need a pen, paper and stopwatch. Follow the instructions for each task and keep to the time limits. Use the score indicators to assess your performance.

Begin preliminary assessment

Test 1: Social/adaptive memory
1.1 Names and faces

Take two minutes to memorize the names and faces of the people illustrated below, then turn the page.

Butch Russell   Pauline Sylvester   Brian Stewart

Bernard Carter   Monica Petrowski   Naomi Bunting

Write down the name of each person.

------------------   ------------------   ------------------

------------------   ------------------   ------------------

How did you do?
Number of faces and names recalled (out of 6):

0–2	3–6	All 6
→ Below average	→ Average	→ Above average

How to improve your performance
Tips for improving attention and concentration are given on pages 100–2. Techniques for remembering names and faces can be found on pages 104 and 123–4. There is more information about social/adaptive memory on pages 137–8.

1.2 Birthdays and anniversaries

Look up the dates of four birthdays and four anniversaries of friends and relatives that you keep forgetting but would like to remember. Take three minutes to relearn them. Then turn the page:

Birthdays

Name   Date

------------------------   ------------------------

------------------------   ------------------------

------------------------   ------------------------

------------------------   ------------------------

Anniversaries

Name   Date

------------------------   ------------------------

------------------------   ------------------------

------------------------   ------------------------

------------------------   ------------------------

After one hour try and recall the dates you have relearnt.

Name   Date
------------------------   ------------------------
------------------------   ------------------------
------------------------   ------------------------
------------------------   ------------------------

------------------------   ------------------------
------------------------   ------------------------
------------------------   ------------------------
------------------------   ------------------------

How did you do?
Number of dates recalled after one hour:

0–2	*3–6*	*More than 6*
→ Below average	→ Average	→ Above average

How to improve your performance
Relearning material is easier than learning from scratch. However, we forget again very rapidly if we fail to rehearse (repeat to ourselves) the information. The more we recall something the less quickly we forget it. Turn to pages 112–13 for information about repetition in learning, and pages 108, 118–22 and 124–9 for techniques for memorizing dates.

1.3 Appointments

Look at this page from a diary showing the planned events of the coming week. Take three minutes to memorize the information, then turn the page.

FEBRUARY

6   **Monday**

1 pm   *Lunch with Annie*

---

7   **Tuesday**

9 am   *Doctor's appointment*   8 pm   *Geoff and Max for dinner*

---

8   **Wednesday**

8.30 am   *School drop*   2 pm   *Meeting at Savoy*

---

9   **Thursday**

9 am   *Research trip to library*

---

10   **Friday**

8.30 am   *School drop*   7.30 pm   *Cinema*

---

11   **Saturday**

2.30 pm   *Children's party*

---

12   **Sunday**

3 pm   *Meet Maddy at Design Museum*

Try and recall the diary entries below:

Monday

Tuesday

Wednesday

Thursday

Friday

Saturday

Sunday

How did you do?

Number of diary entries recalled (out of 10):

0–2	*3–7*	*More than* 7
→ Below average	→ Average	→ Above average

How to improve your performance

See pages 102–4 for tips on bringing organization into your daily life. The method of loci (116–18), pegword systems (118–21) and number-to-code system (126–30) can be adapted to remember a sequence of diary entries.

Test 2: Visual–spatial memory
2.1 Scene

Study the picture below for two minutes. Then turn the page and answer the questions.

1 How many cows are grazing on the hillside?
2 How many trees are there in the scene?
3 Is the car driving away from the walkers?
4 What is the wild animal beside the wood?
5 What has just passed by the church?
6 Who is carrying the backpack of the two walkers?
7 Is the horserider wearing a hat?
8 Are all the cows facing the same way?

Answers

6: The man; 7: Yes; 8: No

1: 4; 2: 8; 3: No; 4: A stag; 5: A cyclist;

How did you do?

Number of questions answered correctly (out of 8):

0–2	*3–6*	*More than 6*
→ Below average	→ Average	→ Above average

How to improve your performance

See pages 100–2 for hints on improving concentration, and page 108 for the method of 'chunking'. An explanation of how to apply chunking to pictures can be found on pages 150–1. There is more information about visual-spatial memory on pages 147–8.

2.2 Abstract drawing

Study the abstract drawing for two minutes. Draw it on a piece of paper if it helps to lodge it in memory. Then turn over the page and recreate the drawing from memory.

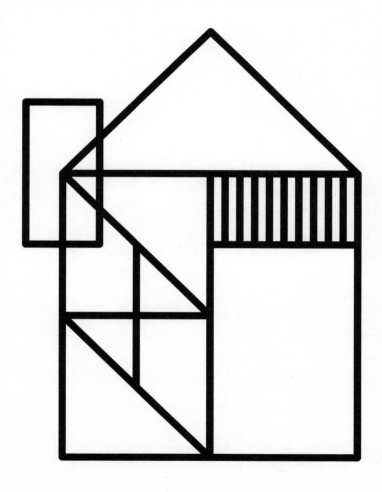

Recreate the drawing from memory here.

How did you do?

Compare your drawing with the original and check the following:

	Yes	No
1 Did you remember the main structure of the figure (the overall shape and main intersecting lines)?		
2 Did you remember more than 50% of the incidental (non-structural) elements?		
3 Did you remember less than 50% of the incidental (non-structural) elements?		

You answered 'no' to questions 1 and 2, and 'yes' to question 3.
→ Below average

You answered 'yes' to question 1 and show a good memory for the structure and organization of visual information. You probably interpreted the structure in terms of an object it reminded you of, for example, a house, which helped you to recall the overall shape. You remembered some of the other details but perhaps not as much as 50%.
→ Average

You answered 'yes' to questions 1 and 2.
→ Above average

How to improve your performance

Abstract drawings are the most difficult to remember. See page 156 for tips on how to remember a drawing and pages 100–2 for tips on improving concentration.

2.3 Mental rotation

Look closely at the cluster of cubes marked A. Then mentally rotate each cube cluster B–E and decide which if any are the same as cube cluster A. There is a time limit of two minutes.

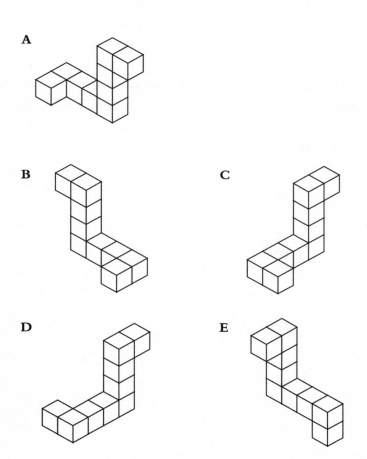

Answer

Cubes C and E are the same as the cube cluster A.

How did you do?

Number of matching cube clusters identified (out of 2):

Zero	*One*	*Two*
→ Below average	→ Average	→ Above average

How to improve your performance

See page 158 for tips on manipulating visual information in your mind. See pages 100–2 for tips on improving concentration.

2.4 Spatial orientation

Memorize the shop floor plan below. After sixty seconds turn the page and answer the questions.

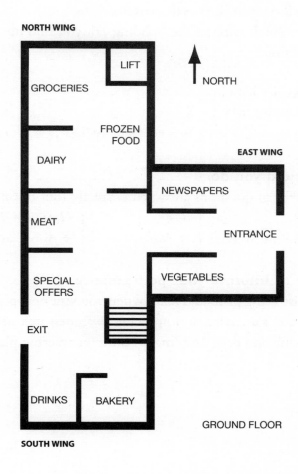

1   Are the stairs opposite the exit?
2   Is the bakery next to the meat section?
3   What is opposite the newspapers in the east wing?
4   Which way does the main entrance face?
5   Is the lift in the north or south wing?
6   In which wing of the building can you find the drinks section?

Answers

1: Yes; 2: No; 3: Vegetables; 4: East; 5: North wing; 6: South wing

How did you do?

Number of questions answered correctly (out of 6):

0–2	3–4	More than 4
→ Below average	→ Average	→ Above average

How to improve your performance

Practise using plans and maps when you visit new places. See page 103 for advice on improving awareness in a new environment, and page 162 for tips on remembering plans.

Test 3: Working memory
3.1 Playing cards

You have two minutes to memorize the cards below. Then turn the page.

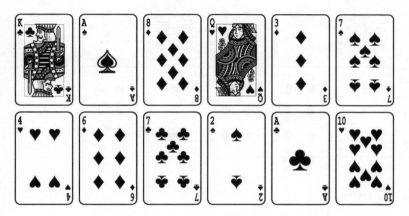

Nine of the twelve cards on the previous page are repeated in exactly the same position below. Which are they?

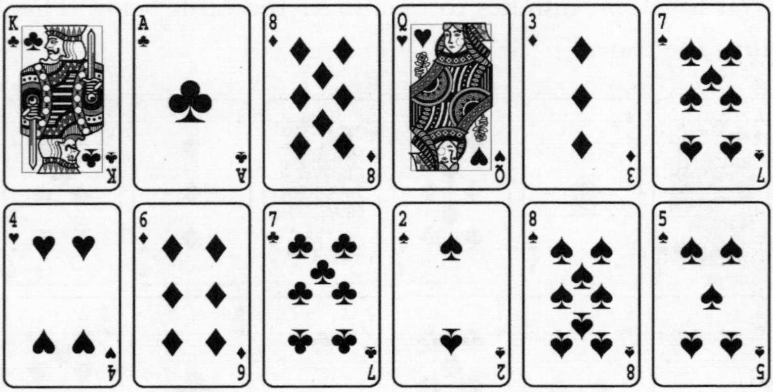

Answers

King and 7 of clubs; 7 and 2 of spades; 8, 6 and 3 of diamonds, queen and 4 of hearts.

How did you do?

Number of cards recognized (out of 9):

0–2	*3–7*	*More than* 7
→ Below average	→ Average	→ Above average

How to improve your performance

See pages 100–2 for tips on improving concentration, pages 126–30 for a system to remember cards, and further tips on page 166. There is more information on working (short-term) memory on pages 80–4 and 163–4.

3.2 Word pairs

You have sixty seconds to memorize the word pairs below, then turn the page.

1	Computer	Banana
2	Paper	Button
3	Monkey	Car
4	Window	Tree
5	Elephant	Water
6	Table	Lollipop
7	Clock	Green
8	Pencil	Wardrobe
9	Book	Picture
10	Lion	Orange

Now write down the paired word associated with each of the following:

1	Computer	----------------------------------
2	Paper	----------------------------------
3	Monkey	----------------------------------
4	Window	----------------------------------
5	Elephant	----------------------------------
6	Table	----------------------------------
7	Clock	----------------------------------
8	Pencil	----------------------------------
9	Book	----------------------------------
10	Lion	----------------------------------

How did you do?
Number of paired words recalled (out of 10):

0–5	*6–9*	*All 10*
→ Below average	→ Average	→ Above average

How to improve your performance
See page 110 for information about forming visualizations and associations, and pages 168–9 for guidance on associated pair learning. Mnemonic systems for remembering lists of items are on pages 115–21.

3.3 Reading memory

Read the following passage from *Bleak House* by Charles Dickens, then turn the page and answer the questions without looking back at the text. You have three minutes to complete the whole test.

The marine-store merchant holds the light, and the law-stationer conducts the search. The surgeon leans against the corner of the chimney-piece; Miss Flite peeps and trembles just within the door. The apt old scholar of the old school with his dull black breeches tied with ribbons at the knees, his large black waistcoat, his long-sleeved black coat, and his wisp of limp white neckerchief tied in the bow the Peerage knows so well, stands in exactly the same place and attitude.

There are some worthless articles of clothing in the old portmanteau; there is a bundle of pawnbrokers' duplicates, those turnpike tickets on the road of Poverty; there is a crumpled paper, smelling of opium, on which are scrawled rough memoranda – as took, such a day, so many grains; took, such another day, so many more – begun some time ago, as if with the intention of being regularly continued, but soon left off. There are a few dirty scraps of newspapers, all referring to Coroners' Inquests; there is nothing else.

1   Who conducts the search?

2   Where is Miss Flite?

3   What is in the old portmanteau?

4   What does the crumpled paper smell of?

5   What do the newspapers refer to?

Answers

1: The law stationer; 2: Just within the door; 3: Worthless articles of clothing; 4: Opium; 5: Coroners' Inquests

How did you do?

Number of questions answered correctly (out of 5):

0–2	*3–4*	*All 5*
➔ Below average	➔ Average	➔ Above average

How to improve your performance

See pages 100–2 for advice on improving concentration, page 110 for information on visualization, and the hints for improving reading memory performance on pages 173–4.

Test 4: Factual memory
4.1 Recall of facts

You have sixty seconds to write down the answers to the following questions (the answers are on the next page):

1   What are the dates of the First World War?
2   Name five of the planets of the solar system.
3   What is the capital of Sweden?
4   When was the first landing on the moon?
5   Is Shakespeare's play *Antony and Cleopatra* a tragedy, romance or comedy?

Now look up five new facts that you do not already know. Memorize each fact and record a question that will test your recall in the spaces below. Test yourself in a week's time.

1   --
2   --
3   --
4   --
5   --

Answers
1: 1914-18; **2:** Any of the following: Mercury, Venus, Earth, Mars, Jupiter, Saturn, Uranus, Neptune (Pluto lost its classification of being a planet in 2006); **3:** Stockholm; **4:** 1969; **5:** A tragedy

How did you do?
Number of facts recalled (out of 5):

| *0–2* | *3–4* | *All 5* |
| ➔ Below average | ➔ Average | ➔ Above average |

How to improve your performance
Your score will depend on how recently you learnt the facts and how regularly you have recalled them correctly. It will also depend on your personal interests, age, culture and experience. There is more about factual memory on pages 175–6, and hints for improving your factual memory are on page 179. For mnemonic methods for storing facts see pages 115–30.

4.2 Definitions

Read the definitions and produce the target words as quickly as possible (the answers are on the following page). You have sixty seconds to complete the test.

Definition	Target word
1 A game in which one person jumps, with legs spread wide, over the bent back of another person.	-------------------
2 A person, usually someone residing in another country, with whom a regular exchange of letters is made.	-------------------
3 A line passing through the centre of a circle from one side to the other.	-------------------
4 A public sale at which items are sold, each one going to the highest bid.	-------------------
5 The means of communication provided by newspapers, radio and TV that gives the public news, entertainment, etc.	-------------------

Answers
1: Leapfrog; **2:** Penpal; **3:** Diameter; **4:** Auction; **5:** Media

How did you do?
Number of correct target words (out of 5):

0–2	*3–4*	*All 5*
→ Below average	→ Average	→ Above average

How to improve your performance
See pages 113–15 for tips on retrieving information from long-term memory. Try these techniques especially if you experience the 'tip-of-the tongue' phenomenon (you know the answer but can't think of it at that moment). General advice for learning and memory is on pages 104–13. A mnemonic system for learning new vocabulary can be found on pages 122–3 (the link-word method).

Test 5: Numerical memory
5.1 Mental calculation

Follow the route below, making the required calculations along the way. Do not write anything down. Allow yourself three minutes to complete the test.

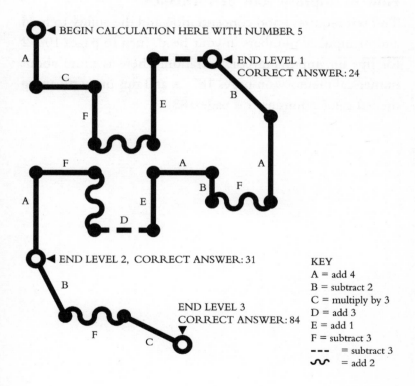

BEGIN CALCULATION HERE WITH NUMBER 5

END LEVEL 1
CORRECT ANSWER: 24

END LEVEL 2, CORRECT ANSWER: 31

END LEVEL 3
CORRECT ANSWER: 84

KEY
A = add 4
B = subtract 2
C = multiply by 3
D = add 3
E = add 1
F = subtract 3
--- = subtract 3
∿ = add 2

How did you do?

| *Calculation error during level 1* → Below average | *Calculation error during level 2* → Average | *Calculation correct up to level 3* → Above average |

How to improve your performance

This test requires good concentration and the ability to hold and manipulate numbers in your head. Turn to pages 100–2 for tips on improving concentration. There is more about numerical memory on pages 182–3, and tips on performing mental calculations are on page 188.

5.2 Telephone numbers

See if you can recall the following:

Your mobile phone number

The telephone number of a friend

A business telephone number

Now write down two useful telephone numbers you would like to learn, for example, the number of a friend, your bank, your doctor's surgery, the garage or the school. Allow yourself sixty seconds to memorize both numbers, then turn the page.

Name   Number

--------------------   ----------------------------------

--------------------   ----------------------------------

Wait five minutes before writing down the numbers you just memorized. Keep testing yourself regularly to lodge them in long-term memory.

Name   Number

-------------------   -----------------------------------

-------------------   -----------------------------------

How did you do?

Recall of telephone numbers learnt in the past (out of 3):

None	*1–2*	*All 3*
→ Below average	→ Average	→ Above average

Recall of telephone numbers newly memorized (out of 2):

None	*1*	*2*
→ Below average	→ Average	→ Above average

How to improve your performance

Do not learn too many telephone numbers at the same time to avoid confusing them. Keep rehearsing the numbers in your head. Try using the method of 'chunking' (see page 108) to help you hold more information in working (short-term) memory. Mnemonic techniques for remembering numbers are on pages 120–2 (narrative pegwords and number-shape system) and 126–30 (number-to-code system).

Test 6: Verbal and auditory memory
6.1 Word manipulation

You have six minutes to answer the following questions. Do not use reference material such as a dictionary, encyclopedia or thesaurus, and do not write anything down except the answers.

1 If the word TIME is written under the word PLAY and the word COPE is written under the word TIME and the word FACE is written under the word COPE, is the word PIPE formed diagonally?

2 In a language called PILEEY, 'PEL PAL POP' means 'He hates honey', 'PIL POL POP' means 'He is sad', 'PUL PIL PEL' means 'Honey is sweet'. Deduce how you would say 'He is sweet' in PILEEY from the clues above. The word order is unimportant.

3 Do the consonants in the word COUSIN appear in alphabetical order?

4 In the English alphabet, how many letters are there between the letters D and M?

5 If you remove eight letters from the word PARENTHESIS, can the word HEART be formed?

6 If all Tilbobs are Spobs and most Tilbobs are Bools, the statement that many Spobs are Bools is:
A. True   B. False
C. Indeterminable

(test continues over the page)

7 Which of the following words is closest in meaning to 'gruesome':

A. Infected   B. Shameful

C. Grisly   D. Pathetic

8 Which of the following words is closest in meaning to 'nonsensical':

A. Exaggerated   B. Unexpressive

C. Trite   D. Unintelligible

Answers

6: A; 7: C; 8: D

1: Yes; 2: POP PIL PUL; 3: No; 4: 8; 5: No;

How did you do?

Number of correct answers (out of 8):

0–2	3–6	*More than 6*
→ Below average	→ Average	→ Above average

How to improve your performance

See the hints on pages 192–3. For more information about verbal and auditory memory see pages 189–90.

6.2 Word lists

Take sixty seconds to memorize the following list of fourteen words, in any order. Then turn the page.

1	Cat
2	Drawer
3	Wall
4	Rain
5	Lake
6	Wheel
7	Grain
8	Wagon
9	Town
10	Cloud
11	House
12	Yellow
13	Chin
14	Penguin

Write down as many words as you can remember in any order. Try the test again after five minutes.

1	---------------------	8	----------------------
2	---------------------	9	----------------------
3	---------------------	10	----------------------
4	---------------------	11	----------------------
5	---------------------	12	----------------------
6	---------------------	13	----------------------
7	---------------------	14	----------------------

How did you do?
Number of words remembered correctly (out of 14):

0–4	*5–9*	*More than 9*
➜ Below average	➜ Average	➜ Above average

How to improve your performance
Techniques for learning lists of words are on pages 115–20. See also the tips on page 196. Practise memorizing lists in everyday life, such as 'to do' and shopping lists.

End of preliminary assessment

Memory questionnaire

Keep a diary for several weeks to identify any memory problems you may have and the frequency of recurrence. Then complete this questionnaire.

Do you have problems with any of the following?

1 Forgetting where things have been placed.

❑ Yes

❑ No

❑ Sometimes

Tips, techniques and tests that could help you

➜ General rules for memory p. 100–15

➜ Working memory tests p. 163–9

➜ Visual-spatial memory tests p. 147–62

2 Forgetting people's names, faces, birthdays, anniversaries, or how to behave in everyday social situations.

❑ Yes

❑ No

❑ Sometimes

Tips, techniques and tests that could help you

➜ General rules for memory p. 100–15

➜ Social/adaptive memory tests p. 137–46

➜ Visual-spatial memory tests p. 147–62

➜ Face-name recognition tips p. 104

➜ Face-name association p. 123–4

(questionnaire continues over the page)

3 Forgetting what has been said.

❏ Yes

❏ No   *Tips, techniques and tests that could help you*

❏ Sometimes   → General rules for memory p. 100–15

                        → Working memory tests p. 163–9

                        → Verbal and auditory memory tests p. 189–96

4 Forgetting telephone numbers.

❏ Yes

❏ No   *Tips, techniques and tests that could help you*

❏ Sometimes   → General rules for memory p. 100–15

                        → Working memory tests p. 163–9

                        → Numerical memory tests p. 182–8

                        → Techniques p. 108, 120–2, 126–30

5 Forgetting what you have read.

❏ Yes

❏ No   *Tips, techniques and tests that could help you*

❏ Sometimes   → General rules for memory p. 100–15

                        → Working memory tests p. 163–9

                        → Factual memory tests p. 175–81

6 Getting lost.

❏ Yes

❏ No   *Tips, techniques and tests that could help you*

❏ Sometimes   → General rules for memory p. 100–15

                        → Visual-spatial memory tests p. 147–62

                        → Spatial orientation tips p. 103

7 Telling the same story too many times.

❑ Yes

❑ No *Tips, techniques and tests that could help you*

❑ Sometimes ➜ General rules for memory p. 100–15

➜ Social/adaptive memory tests p. 137–46

➜ Working memory tests p. 163–9

➜ Factual memory tests p. 175–81

➜ Verbal and auditory memory tests p. 189–96

8 Finding films, books or articles difficult to follow.

❑ Yes

❑ No *Tips, techniques and tests that could help you*

❑ Sometimes ➜ General rules for memory p. 100–15

➜ Verbal and auditory memory tests p. 189–96

➜ Factual memory tests p. 175–81

➜ Techniques p. 109–11, 116–18

9 Missing appointments or being late.

❑ Yes

❑ No *Tips, techniques and tests that could help you*

❑ Sometimes ➜ General rules for memory p. 100–15

➜ Social/adaptive memory tests p. 137–46

➜ Techniques p. 99, 118–20, 126–30

(questionnaire continues over the page)

10 Forgetting lists of things to do or buy.

❑ Yes

❑ No   *Tips, techniques and tests that could help you*

❑ Sometimes   ➜ General rules for memory p. 100–15

                        ➜ Techniques p. 116–20

11 Forgetting facts in exams.

❑ Yes

❑ No   *Tips, techniques and tests that could help you*

❑ Sometimes   ➜ General rules for memory p. 100–15

                        ➜ Memory retrieval tips p. 113–15

                        ➜ Techniques p. 115–30

Your memory weaknesses

Use your test scores and the memory questionnaire to identify any areas of weakness in your memory functioning. List
these in order of priority – the first being the problem that
causes you most anxiety.

1 --
2 --
3 --
4 --
5 --
6 --

A note about motivation

If you are to achieve your memory goals then you must really want to succeed. Without motivation you will almost certainly fail to make the required effort. The more clearly
defined your goals, the more likely they will spur you to
action. For example, your goal may be to pass an exam, or
for a better salary or a new job, or you may consider that
improving memory is important in your case for relationships at home or at work. Much research points to the fact
that having a strong personal motivation greatly enhances
your chance of success. Keep this in mind as you work
through the book.

Reasons to improve your memory

Now list the main reasons why you would like to improve your memory, the first being the most important.

1 --
2 --
3 --
4 --
5 --

Your memory objectives

Use the information from your list of memory weaknesses and your reasons to improve your memory to state your memory objectives. Write down when you would like to achieve these objectives. Keep referring to them and make sure you are working towards your goal.

Memory objectives	Target date
--	------------
--	------------
--	------------
--	------------
--	------------

2

AN INTRODUCTION TO MEMORY TRAINING

Beginning with the ancient Greeks

Before the invention of the printing press, a trained memory capable of storing large amounts of information was of vital importance. The earliest recorded memory training systems date back to the ancient Greeks, who used an elaborate series of techniques known generally as 'mnemotechnics', after Mnemosyne, the mother of the Muses. Inherited by the Romans, and passed down through the Western European tradition, mnemotechnics (or 'mnemonics' as the discipline came to be known) continues to be taught and valued today. Many of the memory training methods described in chapter four of this book derive from those early principles set down for us by the ancient Greeks.

There are just three classical sources that tell us about the principles of mnemonics. The first, by Cicero in his *De oratore* dating from 55 BC, relates an unusual story about a poet named Simonides, the so-called inventor of the art of memory. The story goes that Simonides was invited to chant a lyric poem at a banquet hosted by a Thessalonian nobleman named Scopas, to whom the poem was to be dedicated. Simonides accepted the invitation, but when he chanted his poem he dedicated the verse not only to his host, Scopas, but also to the twin gods Castor and Pollux. Scopas was deeply offended and refused to pay the whole sum agreed; he insisted that half should come from Castor and Pollux as they had also benefited from the poem. During the same evening, two young men called by the nobleman's house asking to see Simonides. The poet stepped outside to speak to the visitors but they were nowhere to be seen. While he was outside the roof of the banqueting hall collapsed with a terrible crash, crushing to death all the occupants. Simonides' life had been spared, and this was his considerable reward from the two young men, who were of course Castor and Pollux. The relevant point of the story is how Simonides applied his memory to the situation. Although the corpses were mangled to be unrecognizable, Simonides was able to help the relatives identify the bodies because he could remember the seating places of each guest in the banqueting hall. The experience led Simonides to think about the art of memory. Realizing his memory of the room's seating arrangement was how he had been able to identify the bodies, he concluded that orderly arrangement is essential for good memory (Yates, 1992).

Between Cicero's account and the other classical sources we are given the rules for systems of memory improvement in classical learning. Memory (*memoria*) in the classical world was one of the skills of rhetoric, the art of using logic and grammar to speak persuasively in public. Roman orators applied the memory aid (mnemonic) of places and images (*loci* and *imagines*) to help them deliver long speeches from memory.

The general rules of this mnemonic involve first memorizing a sequence of locations (*loci*), such as the separate parts, rooms or spaces of a building, and the contents inside those spaces. These places are then used as a structure onto which the speech is 'attached'. This is done by 'placing' (in imagination) each section of the speech inside a different room of the building and linking those sections to the rooms through appropriate images (*imagines*). When the orator wishes to recall his speech, he simply 'walks' through the sequence of rooms in his imagination, drawing from each location the associated image representing the fact or idea to be included in his talk. The locations act as prompts for memory: for instance a hallway may be linked to an image of a Roman general the orator wishes to acknowledge in his introduction. The great merit of this method is that it helps the orator to draw from memory the points of his speech in the correct order. The system relies on the fact that order, as Simonides deduced, is important for memory, and visual images provide one of the strongest memory impressions.

Ad Herrenium (c. 80 BC), the second classical source, distinguishes two kinds of memory, the 'natural' memory we are born with and an 'artificial' memory, one that is strengthened by training. The classical text sets out certain rules for *loci*, including the following tips:

→ care must be taken in forming the locations

→ a large number of places will be needed to remember many things

→ every fifth place should be given a distinguishing mark to avoid confusion

→ places should be tranquil and uncrowded to allow concentration

→ places should not all be identical, such as a row of columns all the same.

The third source, Quintilian's *Institutio oratorio* (first century AD), explains how the method works. The mechanism of remembering things by visiting places in imagination rests on a simple fact that we know from everyday experience: a place can prompt us to call up associations in memory. For example, a visit to a certain seaside resort can bring back memories associated with that place – a person we met there previously, or simply the smell of the sea.

Medieval and Renaissance memory training

Despite the evolving habit of writing things down in manuscripts and books, classical memory systems continued to be handed down through the medieval and Renaissance periods. In medieval Western Europe, under the influence of Christian theology, systems became more pious and concerned with how to live ethically, in particular with remembering virtues and vices. The approach is summed up by Thomas Aquinas, who records that it is only by looking upon the past that we can be directed to do the right thing in the present or future.

The invention of the printing press in 1436 made memory systems less vital as books began to take the place of memory in many spheres of educational and cultural life. However, the new professional class – travelling philosophers, theologians, jurists, merchants, and so on – were increasingly interested in the potential benefits of having a trained memory: they saw it as providing a competitive advantage over those who had to rely on notes and other records to remember things. Their interest provoked a proliferation of printed material on memory systems used for memorizing almost anything. An important milestone during this period was Peter of Ravenna's book, the *Phoenix, sive artificiosa memoria*, the most widely distributed of the memory books of the era (first printed in Venice, 1491). His book refines the principles for the method of loci with practical advice for choosing memory *loci*. The best location for tranquillity, Peter suggests, is an unfrequented church, within which the first place you might position an image (*imagines*) is the door, the second five or six feet further in, and so on.

By the sixteenth century, memory training, rather than becoming a lost art, had entered a new lease of life, taken up by the philosophers of the Renaissance. *The Memory Theatre* of Giulio Camillo became a famous example of the time. A new kind of memory system, this was based on the classical tradition but with Camillo's own curious twist. He built a small wooden theatre and packed it with a variety of images representing objects in the universe from basic elements, through mankind's creation, to human activities in the arts, sciences, religion and law. Reversing the purpose of a theatre, it placed the spectator on the stage, gazing at the images positioned where the seats would have been. The images, representing the order of the universe and the connections between its various parts, provided the *loci* – where things to be remembered could be located in the imagination. The theatre doubled as a system of memory places to help memorize things and a kind of encyclopedia – a quick guide to the constituent parts of the universe.

Modern memory systems

Though not as widely used as in the past, memory systems are still relied upon today by many people in a great variety of professions. In fact, many of us use memory systems without even being aware of them. Modern memory training systems share the principles of their classical predecessors, as you will see when you read chapter four.

A common complaint about memory systems is that their application doesn't suit fast, modern-day life, as there is rarely enough time to learn the techniques. Though this might be true of some of the more complicated systems, many people who have taken the trouble to learn and practise a memory technique consider that the time invested was worthwhile because of the benefits. Another common complaint is that in using visual associations to remember things, it is particularly difficult to find images to remember abstract material. An object such as a dog or a cat is easier to visualize than abstract concepts such as justice or compromise. There are ways to get round this. Abstract words can usually be associated with something concrete, for which there is an obvious image. Alternatively, verbal mnemonics can be used instead of visual techniques. For example, 'Richard of York Gave Battle In Vain' is a verbal mnemonic in which the initial letters of the words correspond with the initial letters of the colours of the rainbow. A third criticism of mnemonic systems is that they provide prompts for remembering lists and general points but are unhelpful for remembering something verbatim, such as a poem. This highlights one of the limitations of memory systems, but on the other hand a prompt can very often be all that is needed to recall a poem or speech with word-for-word accuracy.

Scientific research into mnemonics as an aid to learning and memory is attracting the attention of an increasing number of educators, psychologists and other scientists. There have been positive results in a number of tests. For example, research has shown how subjects of all ages who were taught mnemonic strategies for learning word lists were able to improve their performance in memory tasks (Baltes & Kliegl, 1992). Work by Endel Tulving and others on the process of retrieval of information from memory has contributed to our understanding of how mnemonic methods can aid memory, in particular the importance of making associations. When we learn two pieces of information together, tests show that our recall of one piece of information will prompt the recall of the other associated piece of information. For example, when two words 'computer' and 'banana' are learnt at the same time and associated together in memory using a visual association, then the act of calling up one word (computer) will also retrieve the memory of the other, associated word (banana). Known as 'associated pair' learning, this process underlies mnemonic systems. More generally, mnemonics involve the organization of material to be memorized and encourage us to pay attention to what is being learnt. Numerous studies have shown that both these actions are helpful for memory and learning.

3

THE MEMORY PROCESS

Plato's influential hypothesis

For many years, the wax tablet hypothesis made by the Greek philosopher Plato in the fourth century BC served as a general model for understanding memory. Plato hypothesized that the mind receives impressions from outside in a similar way that a wax tablet is marked when a pointed stick is applied to its surface. A mark on wax eventually disappears as the wax is rubbed smooth again. Plato thought that the same process occurs for memory: an impression, or memory, wears away until eventually it disappears, which is when we forget. Memory and forgetting in Plato's model are two parts of the same process.

Today, most scientists believe that memory and forgetting are two separate processes. Following the work of James (1890), we also believe there is more than one type of memory store: short-term memory, which holds information for only a short period, typically up to 30 seconds long; and long-term memory, which can store information for anything from 30 seconds to a lifetime. A third type of memory is added to many modern theories: sensory memory, a store that receives information from the environment – through vision, hearing, touch, taste and feel. This information stays in the sensory memory store for around 300 milliseconds before it is forgotten or transferred to short-term memory.

The three stages of the memory process

Through the ages, metaphors used for understanding memory have ranged from Plato's wax tablet impressions through an explosion of technology-based metaphors in the nineteenth century associated with recording and sensing things – photographs, phonographs, flashbulbs – to the modern-day popular comparison between brains and computers. Currently, the most influential metaphor or model for memory (though not without its critics) remains the information-processing approach, which sees memory in terms of the operations involved in the processing of information by computers: encoding, storage and retrieval. Applied to the memory process, these three stages work as follows:

→ Encoding is how we acquire new memories and involves registering a piece of information – a visual image, a sound, a fact – and transforming it into a form that allows it to enter into memory.

→ Storage is the retention or 'filing' of information in memory. How we store information affects how efficiently it is recalled. We know that information stored in an organized way and associated with meaningful information already stored is easier to remember.

→ Retrieval is the operation of extracting information

from memory. There are two types of retrieval: recall and recognition. An example of recall is remembering what you did an hour ago, or last week, or where you were ten years ago. Another example is remembering a fact of general knowledge or someone's name. An example of recognition is remembering which house you live in, or answering a multiple-choice question in an exam. Recognizing something is generally easier to do than recalling something.

Development of modern theories

Systematic scientific investigation into memory began over a century ago with the work of Ebbinghaus (1885). Using a simplified memory task under controlled conditions Ebbinghaus found that information loss from memory is rapid after first learning, and then levels off. Much of the research on memory has gravitated between Ebbinghaus's insistence on simplification and the efforts of Bartlett (1932) to model the complexities of memory – its inseparable links with learning, meaning and the fact that no two observers' perception and memory of something are the same.

Models of memory from the 1960s are usually represented by Atkinson and Shiffrin's multi-store model (1968 and 1971), which attempts to explain the flow of information from a short-term memory system to a long-term memory system. This supposes that information is taken in from the environment briefly into a sensory memory store – through seeing, hearing, smelling, tasting or feeling something – from where it goes into a short-term memory store. In short-term memory (or 'working memory') several pieces of information can be held in the conscious mind simultaneously for short periods of time. From here the information is either forgotten or, when we process it for longer-term storage, it moves into long-term memory.

In current theorizing, most scientists accept that a more helpful view of short-term and long-term memory is not of two distinct storage systems, but two different phases of a continuous process. The working-memory model (Baddeley & Hitch, 1974) builds on Atkinson and Shiffrin's multi-store model by attempting to explain some of the complexities of memory. In particular, it shows how information can flow not only from short-term to long-term memory but also in the opposite direction: from long-term to short-term memory. This occurs, for example, when we draw down existing knowledge from long-term memory in order to interpret a new piece of information that has come into our conscious (short-term) memory – as you are doing now in order to interpret the meaning of this sentence.

Working memory

Working memory (also known as 'short-term memory' or 'conscious memory') is central to understanding and improving memory. It plays a crucial role in determining your ability to remember a phone number long enough to dial it, to understand what someone is saying, or to make a calculation in your head. It is the system that allows us to simultaneously hold and manipulate information in consciousness. Using this temporary store of limited capacity you can consciously interrelate information coming in from outside via sensory memory (words, numbers, images, sounds, smells, etc) with information drawn from long-term memory (your existing knowledge and remembered experiences) in order to make sense of things, to reason, and to learn. It is where your thoughts are actively processed. Cohen (1990) describes working memory as 'the focus of consciousness – it holds the information you are consciously thinking about now'.

In the working-memory model developed by Baddeley and Hitch (1974) there are several components to working memory: a function that holds visual and spatial information (an 'inner eye' or 'visuo-spatial sketch pad'); a component for holding verbal information (an 'inner voice', the 'phonological loop', which allows you to rehearse or repeat words in your head); and a central executive function that generally controls the working memory components and relates them to long-term memory. The components of working memory are used to hold information while it is being processed for long-term memory storage, or 'encoded', a process that involves transforming 'raw' information into memorable visual or verbal codes, and rehearsing the codes so you remember them.

Research has shown that the inner voice function that allows you to say things in your head is crucial for language acquisition – both for normal first language development and for learning a second or third language. It allows you to practise words in your head, to 'hear' the sound of them before you utter them out loud. The inner eye function that allows you to display and manipulate visual information in your mind is used to 'see' things you want to 'inspect' in imagination. For example, someone asked about the colour of the eyes of their dog (when the dog isn't present) may, if they have a good visual memory, be able to think up a mental image of the dog and then zoom in to 'look' at the eyes.

It is generally accepted that the normal working memory of an adult holds around seven pieces of information at any one time. Exactly what constitutes a 'piece of information' depends on how the information is taken in by the learner. For example, someone who remembers digits one by one may have a working memory capacity of around seven digits. On the other hand, a person who 'chunks' together digits into groups of twos or threes and relates the groups of digits using rhythm and sound may enlarge his working memory capacity beyond the normal seven digits. The same applies for remembering a list of words. By organizing the words into types you can usually hold more than seven words in working memory. 'Chunking' information is a process we have learned to do naturally in language, when we group or 'chunk' together letters into words, words into phrases and phrases into sentences (Miller, 1956). In memory processing, some people naturally 'chunk' information together; others need to practise and learn to organize information in this way. It is a skill worth acquiring: by giving information a structure it does not already have, larger amounts of information can be dealt with in short-term memory at the same time. This is a very effective method for increasing memory processing power and, by extension, mental capacity.

Another way to measure short-term memory span is to count how long on average an item stays within working memory before it is forgotten. The normal range for adults is between ten and thirty seconds.

How we store information in working memory

For information to enter working memory it first must be registered. If you are distracted when exposed to information, then nothing will reach the working memory store. For example, on entering a room at a party, it is easy to instantly forget new names if you are distracted when introduced to people. This represents a failure in the encoding process.

When encoding is successful, you register the information by paying attention to it when it is first introduced to you and you keep it active in your consciousness. Keeping it active involves rehearsing the information (repeating it to yourself). It helps if you pay attention to the sound and rhythm of the words, if you organize the information in your mind, as you would organize or group the digits of a telephone number into twos or threes, and if you make an association with something you already know. It also helps if you visualize an object soon after looking at it, and if you can interact with it – through touch, taste or speech. For example, on meeting a man called 'Mr Panister', it can help to hold his name in consciousness if you notice the sound and pronunciation of 'Panister' and repeat the word in conversation. If you also visualize meeting Mr Panister while standing by a 'banister' (which rhymes with 'Panister') you may succeed in holding his name in memory for longer. Later on when you recall the image of him beside the banister this should prompt you to remember his name.

Long-term memory

When people talk about improving their memory they are usually referring to the storage and retrieval of information from long-term memory. The duration of memories in long-term memory storage is not known. Some scientists believe memories remain permanently, but they become inaccessible to recall; others believe that memory traces gradually fade over time or are overwritten by new information coming in. Unlike information in working memory, information in long-term memory is not consciously accessible until it is recalled and moved back into working, or short-term, memory.

Long-term memory is made up of several components:

→ Episodic memory – information about who we are and the personal events of our lives (our names, where we come from, what we did last year, etc).

→ Prospective memory – our plans for the future, from keeping an appointment to life plans.

→ Semantic memory – knowledge about the world, including facts such as the capital of Chile (Santiago), the meaning of a sentence or the biological function of the kidneys; and sensory knowledge such as knowing the smell of the sea or the taste of butter.

→ Procedural memory – knowledge of how to do things, like riding a bicycle or driving a car, that once learnt brings about automatic and conditioned behaviour: experienced drivers don't have to think consciously about how to drive a car, they do it automatically.

How we store information in long-term memory

Information enters long-term memory through the process of encoding. During this process, it makes a more durable memory, and one more easily recalled, if the information is organized systematically and linked to things we already know. This is like placing a memory in the right filing cabinet, drawer and file so you find it again easily at a later date. If stored correctly, you are more likely to retrieve the memory. If stored in the wrong place, it can be lost forever.

A good deal of memory encoding occurs naturally at a sub-conscious level, but the point of memory training is to carry out more encoding at a conscious level so you choose how to store the information. For example, when learning a new fact, you may choose to encode (or 'label') the information by creating a new 'file' specifically for the fact you want to remember, or you may choose to place it with a piece of information already in memory, by association.

Studies suggesting that related information is stored together in memory include work by Bousfield (1953), who demonstrates how we tend to recall words and facts in clusters. From a memory test consisting of a list of random words, he shows how we cluster items into categories, for instance, by grouping together all the animal words, vegetable words, people's names, etc.

A useful model for imagining how information is stored in semantic memory is the hierarchical network model (Collins & Quillian, 1969, 1972). In this, the information in memory is seen as a hierarchical structure of multiple, interconnected associations and pathways linking concepts and their relationships with one another. For example, the concept 'animal' is associated with the concepts 'dog' and 'cat' on lower tiers in the hierarchy. These concepts in turn are associated with others like 'labrador' and 'abyssinian', and these in turn with concepts such as 'colour black', 'stout', 'happy temperament', 'highly intelligent' and so on. In effect, each memory 'contains thousands of… concepts, each with very many connections, so that the actual topographical representation would look like a huge "wiring diagram"' (Bower & Hilgard, 1981).

Part of the encoding process involves attaching a visual image or smell or sound to information to make it more memorable (Robertson-Tchabo, 1980). For example, a trip to the seaside becomes instantly more memorable if we 'attach' the smell of the sea, the sound of the seagulls, the texture of the sand. All the senses can be used to reinforce memories but numerous studies show that visual images are particularly important in forging memories – and by extension, in memory improving skills (West & Crook, 1992). In the latter, visual imagery can help us to remember numbers, random lists of items, sequences of events and a host of other items that many people find difficult to memorize. Actions also help memory, for example, the act of writing things down.

Encoding information using imagery should not be confused with a perceptual phenomenon known as eidetic imagery, a photographic memory facility which some children have. This involves a persistent image in memory from which the child can recall detail with astonishing accuracy. In rare cases the condition extends into adulthood.

Depth of processing

In 1972, Craik and Lockhart added an influential twist to our understanding of how information is processed for storage in long-term memory. They suggested that the durability of memories depends on how 'deeply' we process the information during learning. Deeper processing involves categorizing information in terms of colours and textures, sounds, and other sensory characteristics, and in particular in terms of its meaning – which is seen as the most important way of categorizing information in order to remember it later. The more varied the categories and senses we employ in processing information, the deeper the encoding and the more likely the memory will be recalled. This is because if we use many parts of the brain when we encode a memory, more neural pathways become associated with the memory, thus raising the probability that one or other of those pathways will lead to the memory later on.

Recall

Recalling information from long-term memory involves consciously thinking about one or other of the associations or cues applied during learning. The prompt leads us to the memory we wish to access, which then transfers to working memory, where we become consciously aware of its contents. For example, thinking about a place might prompt us to think about a weekend spent there in the past.

Cues for recall can be words, images, smells, tastes, actions, even rhymes. Rhyming verse has acted as a prompt for remembering nursery rhymes for generations of children; the smell of talcum powder can bring back memories of childhood; seeing a koala may retrieve a memory of a visit to Australia; the taste of burrito, a trip to Mexico; and so on. Recent research has shown that recall is excellent if a subject, in learning something, not only uses several different cues for recall but also performs some activity connected with it. The dense network of neural pathways this creates ensures a particularly durable and accessible memory.

Not all memories are well stored and their retrieval from long-term memory can be difficult. For example, everyone has experienced the 'tip-of-the-tongue' phenomenon when we feel that we know something but we cannot think what it is. This doesn't mean that the information is lost, just that we are unable to retrieve it at a particular moment in time. A common cause for memory blocks such as these is stress or mental fatigue. In this instance, often the best strategy is to go away and relax, then come back to it later. If this fails, we may still succeed in accessing the memory through recognition – by recognizing the information when it is presented to us again – which is easier to do than recall.

Most retrieval failures are due to inadequate processing during storage of memories. If a memory has been stored in the wrong place – categorized according to an incorrect meaning perhaps – then we may never retrieve it, just as someone may never find a book that has been shelved on the wrong shelf in a library. The reason most of us cannot remember events from the first years of our lives seems to be because babies are not good at storing information – they have an inadequate world view to act as a framework on which to attach new memories. There are other reasons for recall failure besides inadequate storage, for example repression of memories due to an emotionally stressful event, chemical influences such as alcohol or drugs, illness or the natural process of ageing.

To avoid retrieval failure, a good approach is to store information in an organized way and call it up at regular intervals using a systematic 'search'. Tulving (1966) and others have shown that the act of retrieving information from memory can contribute to learning – the more we use the retrieval cues to search for a memory, the stronger the route to the memory becomes and the easier it is to retrieve on subsequent occasions. This is why regular testing during learning helps to reinforce learning and recall.

Why we forget

The act of forgetting can actually be a good thing. It allows us to get rid of useless information so we can focus on remembering important information. If we were unable to forget anything, we would remember such things as what we wore each day for the rest of our lives, or, worse still, an event that we would prefer not to be reminded of. Of course, forgetting isn't always useful, when we can't remember things that we want to or should remember. Memory failures that involve forgetting can occur at any of the three steps of the memory process. When given some new information, if we fail to register it because we are distracted then there is nothing to store or retrieve. While encoding and storing information, we may file it in the wrong place so we cannot access it again. Sometimes the information is overwritten or confused with another memory. This happens especially if the old and the new memories are similar and easily mixed up (a process known as 'interference'). The problem often occurs during retrieval: information may have been encoded and stored properly, but we fail to retrieve it because we can't find the right cue. This is probably because we have failed to retrieve the information regularly enough and have forgotten the cues that would lead to it.

The effect of ageing

The optimum age for memorizing information and recall is between sixteen and twenty-three. As we get older, brain processing speeds reduce, affecting memory and other cognitive functions and slowing our response rates. Performance varies widely between individuals, but on average older people may become less good at orientating themselves than they used to be, especially in unfamiliar environments (Rabbit, 1989). Prospective memory tends to worsen, making us more forgetful of plans for the future – such as

keeping appointments – unless we are practised at usin,
diary or a 'to do' list. Access to semantic memory (storing
knowledge about the world) may slow down, and we
become less adaptable at learning new skills and employing
procedural memory. Kemper (1990) has also found a
decrease in working memory capacity, making manipulation
of complex material more difficult – the effects, for instance,
showing up in chess, with older players more likely to make
errors through forgetfulness.

However, there are advantages that can outweigh the
physical effects of ageing. Older subjects with more experience in a particular line of work have advantages over
younger ones doing the same tasks: they generally use more
in-depth analysis, plan further ahead and employ better
techniques and style in their practised disciplines; they also
have greater accumulated knowledge to apply in solving
problems. In addition, older people using mnemonic techniques have been seen to do at least as well as younger subjects in the same memory tests (Baltes & Kliegl, 1992).
Memory techniques especially work to narrow the gap
between memory abilities of old and young if the material
being remembered is richly encoded (Baddeley, 2004). This
means using visual and verbal associations, sound, touch and
taste, and especially action – interacting with an item rather
than simply looking at it.

The best approach to counteract the signs of ageing is to
apply memory-improving techniques (such as those in

chapter four) and to keep the brain active – crossword puzzles, taking up new interests, reading widely, learning a new language and new skills, being open to new ideas, drawing or memorizing pictures can all help.

As we get older, we are more likely to suffer from Alzheimer's disease, the most common form of dementia affecting the elderly. It causes serious and rapid decline in cognitive functions including memory, language, attention, problem solving, orientation and movement. There is still no treatment for Alzheimer's disease, though there are ways to help sufferers, such as training in the use of external memory aids (making lists, using diaries, etc), which can go some way towards maintaining normality in everyday life.

The physical basis of memory

So far we have considered the process of memory – how we take in, store and retrieve information – but how does this translate to the structure of the brain? In the twentieth century, much work was done to understand the physical basis of memory. We now know that no single structure or place in the brain is responsible for memory. The hippocampus (which lies within the temporal lobe of the brain – see overleaf) and the frontal lobe are certainly important in the memory process, but many other areas of the brain are also employed in memory functioning. We know this because damage to a small part of the brain can interfere with some functions of memory and not others.

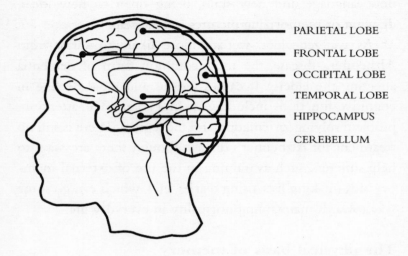

PARIETAL LOBE
FRONTAL LOBE
OCCIPITAL LOBE
TEMPORAL LOBE
HIPPOCAMPUS
CEREBELLUM

It is thought that memories are encoded in long-term memory by chemical changes in specific neurons, although it is also possible that new memories could be formed by the growth of new synapses (the junctions between neurons across which messages flow). Treatment of brain-damaged patients has provided evidence that it is possible to have a defective short-term memory with a normal long-term memory, or vice versa, suggesting that nerve activity in the brain may be different for short-term and long-term memory. This implies that short-term and long-term memory processes are independent of each other and information does not necessarily have to lodge in short-term memory before it transfers to long-term memory, as in the multi-store model proposed by Atkinson and Shiffrin. Memory is clearly a very complex system of electrochemical processes and there is still much work to be done to fully understand its physical basis.

4

TECHNIQUES FOR IMPROVING MEMORY

External memory aids

Learning and remembering things takes time and effort. Rather than trying to remember everything – and failing – get into the habit of using external memory aids such as written lists, tape recorders, diaries, calendars, wall charts and alarm clocks. Lists or prompts around the house – for example, the rubbish placed by the door so you remember to put it out in the morning – are an efficient way to remember practical 'to do' items. Some people believe that relying on external memory aids makes the mind lazy. However, there is no evidence to suggest that their use will hinder memory development. In fact, the organization and routine that external aids bring to your life may even help to improve your memory – you will be less stressed and more able to concentrate when you really do need to commit something to memory.

Internal memory aids

Despite the usefulness of external memory aids, it is often important to be able to remember without them, for example, when studying for an exam, or simply to remember someone's name. This is when internal memory strategies come in useful.

Many of us were taught to remember things by repeating them over and over. Known as learning by rote, this is the strategy we use to remember the multiplication tables or the alphabet, or to memorize telephone numbers or the pronunciation of a foreign phrase. Rote repetition uses the sound and rhythm of word, letter and number sequences to help us remember things but does not in itself aid understanding.

The purpose of this chapter is to introduce a variety of other strategies for learning and remembering things to be used alongside repetition. First there are important general rules that apply to all situations of learning and memory. Then we will turn to some of the main mnemonic systems, the specific memory aids that involve elaborating the meaning of material in order to make it easier to remember.

General rules for memory

There are a few general rules for learning and memory that everyone should practise:

➜ **Maintain attention and concentration:** Memorizing something requires sustained attention (concentration over time). To maintain concentraton try the following: avoid distractions, develop an interest in information to be learnt, recap regularly, break long tasks into manageable portions, repeat what has been said in conversation, read aloud, take frequent breaks and keep healthy.

→ **Organize your life and your learning material:** Organization is the secret of good memory. Bring organization into your life to aid concentration and learning. Organize the material you want to remember to make it more meaningful and therefore more memorable.

→ **Make associations:** Add meaning to information to be remembered by linking it to things you already know and have experienced personally. Transform information into visual images if this helps you to remember.

→ **Understand:** Break down complex information into key points and make sure you understand them. Read widely on the same subject. A thorough understanding of material is often the best strategy for learning.

→ **Rehearse and test:** Rehearse information in your mind to keep it available in working memory, and test yourself at increasing intervals to lodge information in long-term memory. Recalling information helps memory.

All these rules are so important, and so often ignored, that we will look at each one in detail.

Attention and concentration

The first step to remembering something is to absorb information into working (short-term) memory from outside via our senses. This requires attention, and for difficult tasks, sustained attention over time, or concentration. Our senses are bombarded with information, especially in noisy, crowded environments, but we have an important filter that allows into memory only the information that is relevant to our purposes. When we are distracted, or stressed, we may have difficulty registering information that we should be taking in, resulting in poor memory encoding and storage. A lapse in attention or concentration is a major reason for not remembering something.

Attention span can be increased. Practise tasks that require concentration, preferably ones that are progressively more complex, requiring more time to complete, like the tests in this book. Here are some tips for improving your attention and concentration:

Organize your life
Organize your daily life so you can allocate time for learning and time for relaxation. Good daily organization will help you keep track of what you have to do. When organized, you have a greater feeling of control, are less stressed and more able to turn your mind to learning and remembering things. When in control, you are more assertive about requiring a quiet environment for learning.

Focus on one task at a time
If you have several things to do, try to set yourself a time when you should switch to the next task, rather than trying to do two things at the same time. If you are interrupted, make a note of where you got to and what is left to do when you return to the task. If you have trouble focusing your

attention on one thing, choose a quiet environment to complete the task and be firm when asking people to come back later if they want you to do something.

Be aware of your environment

Get into the habit of being aware of your surroundings: taking things in is the first step to remembering them. Practise noticing details you wouldn't normally pay attention to. If you are easily lost in an unfamiliar place, orientate yourself. For example, find out which way is north using a street plan or the position of the sun. Inside a building, make a mental note of which way it faces, the exit points, how many floors there are and the location of lifts and stairs. In the street, notice the names of the roads each time you turn a corner and pick out dominant features of buildings so you recognize them on your return. When you leave your car in a car park, make a mental note of the immediate surroundings.

Keep track of your belongings

If you are in the habit of leaving belongings behind or losing things, establish a routine of consciously checking your actions on leaving or arriving somewhere. For example, think about where you place your bag on arrival, and whether you have picked it up on departure. If you have trouble remembering where you put your keys or other belongings in the home, make a special place for keeping each item and be strict about returning it there.

Alternatively, have one box or drawer where all things you need to take with you on a regular basis are kept. If necessary, make a list of items you need each time you go out. Collect the items together before departure and check them in when you return home. Eventually, preparation for departing somewhere will trigger a mental list.

Remember names and faces

Get into the habit of studying faces, noticing how they fall into visual types and how they differ individually. Practise picking out distinctive features. When introduced to new people, try to block out distractions and give yourself a moment to attend to their features. Repeat their name in conversation and concentrate on the sound to lodge it in auditory memory. Repeat the name and recall the face several times to yourself during the following minutes, hours and days. Each time you recall the name, create a mental picture of the face and the place you first met. Remembering the context of your meeting will prompt your memory. When there are a lot of new names to remember at once, for example at a conference, ask for and study the names of attendants in advance so you recognize them when you are introduced in person. A face-name association technique is described on pages 123–4.

Be motivated

One of the best ways to help concentration and awareness is to have a passionate interest in things. Children learn most if they follow their interests, and it is the same for adults. Motivation causes you to focus your attention and devote extra time to something, whether it is learning a new skill or reading for pleasure. When truly interested in a subject, you will spend hours or days thinking about it and discussing it with friends. In doing so you are forging rich associations with your existing knowledge, which creates deeper and more durable memories. If a topic appears dull, try reading around the subject and finding links to things you already know and enjoy. The best way to develop an interest in something is to be actively involved in it. For example, exchange rates and foreign money markets may be subjects that have never attracted your attention until you need to change money for a trip abroad or import an item from a foreign country. One way to spark an interest in a topic is to search for related stories, discussions and newsworthy events. The Internet is a useful starting point.

Taking in what you hear

During conversation, if what you hear is complex, repeat it in your own words to make sure you understand and to help lodge it in memory. Be assertive and ask people to explain what they mean if they are unclear, or to speak more slowly if you can't keep up. When listening to a talk, concentrate on what is being said rather than trying to write everything down; if you need to make notes later, jot down a few key words as a prompt. Link information to your own experience and interests. If the material raises questions, record a reminder to look up the answer or ask the speaker. In the hours and days that follow, turn over in your mind the main points conveyed and form your own opinion of the piece.

Taking in what you read

Whether studying or reading for pleasure, take a break before your concentration dwindles, and come back refreshed later on. Avoid reading directly after a heavy meal because concentration dips during this period. Find a quiet place where you can think without being disturbed. Pause regularly and recap: rehearse in your mind and in your own words what you have just read. If studying, keep in mind your learning objectives and check at regular intervals that the material is providing the knowledge you need. If possible, read aloud so you can concentrate on what you are hearing as well as what you are seeing on the page.

Little and often

When learning, most people concentrate better and remember more if they work for short periods several times a day rather than for a long stretch once a day. Leave complicated tasks to times when you are at your most wide awake – some people prefer mornings; others work best in the afternoons.

Avoid stress and toxins

Stress is known to affect memory performance and learning. Some positive stress may be good for motivation, but too much and concentration suffers. Alcohol is the most common toxin that has an effect on brain functioning, in particular on memory. Learning how to relax and avoiding stress and toxins will give your body and mind a better chance to function optimally.

Eat well, rest and exercise

Concentration deteriorates when you are tired, and inadequate amounts of sleep can affect memory performance. Missing breakfast or other meals can make access to long-term memory inefficient as blood sugar levels fall. Eating little and often is the best policy for remaining alert. Oily fish, such as salmon, mackerel and tuna, is good for memory and learning and should be eaten at least once a week. Foods rich in vitamins A, C and E are also beneficial. Regular exercise keeps the body healthy and in shape, which has a positive effect on mental concentration.

Organizing material

Organizing material helps us to remember it. For example, we know that if people are asked to recall a shopping list, they remember more when they group the items into categories — like dairy, meat, vegetables, household products — than if they try to remember the list as a random collection of items. If you want to remember something you have read, summarize the key points and organize the material into a memorable structure. Organizing material in your mind is part of the encoding process that transforms raw information entering our brains via our senses into meaningful information that we can remember.

Here are a few organizational strategies for aiding memory:

Chunking

This is a method of organization that involves grouping information into meaningful 'chunks'. For example, telephone numbers are often remembered in chunks of information representing international and local codes. The advantage in remembering a number as 020-8741-3663 instead of 02087413663 is that it is easier to hold three chunks of information in your head than if you try to remember eleven individual digits. The same concept applies to language: we remember letters grouped as words more easily than individual letters because the words (letter-groups) have meaning.

Rhyme and rhythm

Rhythm is important to memory – rhyme, rhythm and repetitive structure are what make poetry easier to memorize than prose, and why nursery rhymes have been remembered and handed down through so many generations. Grouping digits together, for instance the digits of a telephone number, allows you to repeat them rhythmically, which helps reduce the tendency to recall them in the wrong order (Baddeley, 2004). Some of the mnemonic techniques in the following section use rhyme (see page 124).

Categories

When learning a new topic or trying to make sense of information, it helps to remember things if you categorize the material systematically, beginning with general ideas and concepts and working down to finer points. For example, when learning about plants you might first link the topic to related subjects – the plant kingdom in relation to the animal kingdom, for instance – noting the differences and similarities between them. On the next level you could organize information under 'headings' such as 'the structure of a plant', 'how plants reproduce', 'how plants use energy from sunlight in order to grow', 'types of plant', and so on. Under each of these headings you could then highlight key points, such as the 'English name', 'Genus', 'Colour', 'Country of origin' under each plant type, adding further details under each of these points until you reach a level of detail satisfactory for your learning purposes.

Some people prefer to learn the details first and work up to an overall picture. Experiment to find out which method works best for you. The important point is to learn in an organized fashion because structure adds meaning, which helps you to remember things. When you come to recall the information, a mental 'search' of the structure will lead you to the memory you wish to retrieve. Unfortunately, not all material we have to memorize naturally fits an organizational pattern. For remembering random and unrelated items, see the mnemonic techniques in the next section.

Visualization

A useful way to remember is to visualize what is being said or read. This makes it more memorable, especially if the mental image is larger than life and embellished with tastes, colours, textures and sounds. Many people find learning easier if they can hold a picture in their head of the whole topic. Visualizing the structure of the topic acts as a prompt for recreating individual parts of the subject from the whole.

Associations

Crucial to learning and remembering is the meaningfulness of information to the learner (Baddeley, 2004). Linking new information to something you already know or have experienced personally makes it more meaningful to you, and therefore easier to remember: the association between new and existing knowledge becomes forged in memory so that calling up one item brings up the other. For example, you may remember that the spelling of 'stationery' has an 'e' in it because you put stationery (a letter) inside an envelope. Or you may associate the name of your new doctor with a friend of the same name. Many people use visualizations to reinforce associations. For example, to remember to take a file with you in the morning, you may visualize it lying on top of your briefcase – so when you see your case you remember the associated file. Mnemonic systems rely heavily on associations and visualizations to link information.

Senses

All our senses are powerful memory stimulants. Think about the memories that are associated with the smell of baby powder, the sound of a church bell, the feel of seaweed or the taste of champagne. When you want to remember important information, use as many senses as possible to process it, for example, visualize it, listen to people speaking about it, read articles, write about it. To remember an object or place, analyse it in terms of its appearance, smell, taste, sound and texture. The richer the variety of senses used to process information, the more likely you are to retrieve it from memory.

Summarize

Cutting out superflous information helps learning. One way to do this is to break down complex information into essential points, then reduce these to key words. Key words act as prompts to retrieve the important points. Use this strategy when making notes instead of trying to write everything down. Put the key words in the middle of a piece of paper with lines radiating out to related points and themes. Keep returning to your summary to be sure you can reconstruct the original material from the points you picked out. Each time you do this you are reinforcing your memory. Practise this procedure for remembering details of films, papers, articles, stories, etc.

Repetition and practice

In addition to applying organizational strategies, memorizing and learning require rehearsal (repetition) and testing. These ensure that we use the information before it is forgotten, which in turn helps to lodge it in long-term memory.

Rehearsal for short-term memory

Repeating information in your mind or aloud is a method used to retain information in working (short-term) memory long enough for it to be encoded and then stored in long-term memory. For example, if you want to remember a number long enough to transfer it from an address book to the number key pad on the telephone, mental repetition is the technique you would use. If, at the same time, you focus on the meaning of the information, you can store more in working memory for the same amount of effort – for example, repeating a telephone number while focusing on the 'chunks' of information that represent area code and the rest of the number (see 'chunking' on page 108).

Expanded rehearsal for long-term memory

Many students make the mistake of failing to practise recalling information during learning, which is why facts memorized for exams are so often forgotten soon afterwards. When storing information in long-term memory, a useful strategy to improve your chances of retrieval later on is the expanded rehearsal technique. This involves testing yourself immediately after learning, then at increasing intervals, for example, 30 seconds later, 1 minute later, 5 minutes later, 15 minutes, 30 minutes, 1 hour, 3 hours, 12 hours, 2 days, 1 week, 3 weeks, and so on. After Landauer and Bjork (1978) it is important to correct errors at each testing. If, at any point, recall fails, then relearn and decrease the interval between testing until you can increase the delay again without making a mistake. Keep relearning material even if you think you know it already. It creates deeper memory impressions, ensuring the memories are accessible for longer.

Avoid learning similar things at the same time

Learning similar pieces of information at the same time can result in confusion between the two. This is known as interference and is a main cause of forgetting – new information coming in simply replaces the old, especially if the information is similar. Try not to work at the same time on topics that may be confused. For example, learning two languages at once or two lists of similar items. If you have to learn similar things together, use an external memory aid to reinforce your memory of at least one of them.

Tips for recall

Retrieval of information from long-term memory can sometimes prove difficult. The 'tip-of-the-tongue' phenomenon occurs when you have learnt something but cannot recall it when needed, though you feel frustratingly close to it. When this happens there are several things you can do to help recall:

Run through the alphabet

Sometimes the first letter of a name or word may lead you to remember the whole name so try running through the alphabet testing each letter in turn.

Return to the original context of learning

Studies have shown that memory retrieval is easier when you are in the same place as you were when the information was first learnt. For example, if you recognize a face but cannot place the person, try returning in your mind to places where you may have met. If you are trying to recall a book, imagine yourself in the same seat as when you first read it. If possible, remember your thoughts that day, the associations you made while reading, the smell of the book, the place, etc. If you have lost something, it often helps to mentally retrace your movements back to when you rememeber using it last.

The mood we are in may influence our ability to remember. In general, things learnt when we are sober are better recalled when we are sober. Although memory deteriorates when we drink alcohol, it is also the case that things remembered when we are drunk may be remembered better when we are in a similar state again. The same can be said for emotions of happiness and sadness. If the original emotion experienced when we learnt something can be re-experienced it may help recall.

Relaxation

Sometimes, simply relaxing and returning to the information later helps to remove a mental block.

Mnemonic systems

Mnemonics are memory aids that organize information in a special way to aid learning and memory. Derived from principles introduced by the ancient Greeks, typically they add meaningful associations between what is being learnt and what is already known and stored in long-term memory (Belezza, 1981).

Mnemonics tend to make information more elaborate, resulting in more information rather than less, but information that is easier to store in memory and recall. Most of us have used mnemonics at some stage in our lives. For example, many people use a first letter mnemonic 'Every Good Boy Deserves Favour' for learning musical notes on the lines of the stave.

Higbee (2001) distinguishes between visual mnemonic systems (using imagery) and verbal mnemonic techniques (making associations with words). The use of imagery can be traced to the Greek Simonides, who invented the principle behind the method of loci, a mnemonic popular since classical times. This principle involves associating or 'hanging' new information onto a piece of existing knowledge (a location) in order to make the new information easier to recall. The location is used to access the new information associated with it – visualizing the location acts as a prompt to recall the associated information (see pages 67–70). Other mnemonics described in this section work on similar principles of association and cues for recall. Most of them can be used to remember lists of items, long numbers and facts. Numbers are about the hardest things to remember because they are abstract and not concrete; by relating them to words or pictures they become more meaningful and therefore easier to recall. Which system you use depends on personal preference. The best thing is to try a few and settle on one or two that you find work the best.

Don't forget that you still need to practise repetition to strengthen the links formed by mnemonic methods.

Visual mnemonics
These techniques rely on interactive visual impressions to tie one piece of information to another.

Method of loci
This is a useful technique to help recall a list of unrelated items or a speech or article. It involves using previously memorized visual cues (a set of locations) to organize and retrieve newly associated information. First of all visualize a familiar environment, for example, a favourite walk or a sequence of rooms in your own home. Identify at least ten memorable landmarks on the walk or ten rooms or 'stopping points' within each room, such as opposite a window, on top

of the bed, inside the dresser. If you intend to remember more than ten items you will need to increase the number of places or stopping points (to avoid confusion, give every fifth place a distinguishing mark). Then 'walk' around your environment in your mind, visiting each location in turn, until you can recall the sequence without any trouble.

When you want to remember a list of items, imagine each one placed in the locations in the order in which the rooms or features occur. Relate each object to its location using a mental image – one that links the object to the location in a relevant and striking way. Don't be afraid to exaggerate. For example, to remember a list that begins 'wine, apple pie, washing-up liquid' you might imagine opening a new wine bottle-shaped door to your house, nibbling on a giant apple pie in the hallway, finding a sea of detergent bubbles in the kitchen, and so on. Once committed to memory, these images are retrievable by wandering through the house, visiting each room in turn. Use the same method to remember a speech or a talk, picking out key points and relating them to locations. For example, a talk on the subject of 'justice' beginning with a dialogue between Socrates and his student Glaucon might be remembered by imagining the interaction between Socrates and Glaucon taking place in the hallway of your home, and other key details related to different locations in the house. To remember a story or an article using this method, select the key events or points and imagine them re-enacted in different rooms.

A famous user of this method was the Russian journalist Shereshevskii, whose memory appeared vast and involved being able to recall lists of more than one hundred digits and complex scientific formulae, even though he had no scientific training. The method of loci has also been used successfully by brain damaged and elderly people to aid recall. Bower (1972) has shown that on average between twice and seven times more is remembered using this technique. The main drawbacks are that you need to memorize your locations very well and you cannot retrieve an item in your list or speech without running through the sequence of locations in your mind – which can take a little time to do.

Narrative story method

In this modern variation on the method of loci, instead of associating items with fixed locations, they are incorporated into a meaningful story. Retell the story to remember them. This method can be used to remember a list of unrelated items. For example, the list 'wine, apple pie, washing-up liquid' could become a 'mini-story' about having a glass of wine, and experiencing a vision involving an apple pie floating on a green sea of washing-up liquid.

Pegword system

The pegword system is a useful method for memorizing lists of items in the correct order. Instead of locations, it uses a series of words, or 'pegs' on which to attach information.

First choose a set of pegwords to represent numbers one to ten. One option is to use words that are meaningfully linked to numbers. For example, the pegword for 1 could be 'moon', because there is just one moon; 2 could be 'eyes' or 'wings' or 'feet', because there are two of each of these; 3 could be 'stool'; and so on. Alternatively, you can use words that rhyme with numbers, for example, the memorable nursery rhyme, 'This Old Man, he plays One, he plays nick nack on my Thumb...', gives the following pegwords:

> One – Thumb (or Drum)
> Two – Shoe
> Three – Knee
> Four – Door
> Five – Hive
> Six – Sticks
> Seven – Heaven
> Eight – Gate
> Nine – Spine (or Line)
> Ten – Hen
> and add...
> Zero – Nero

Memorize the list by repeating the rhyme – make sure you know it really well. Then to use the pegwords to remember ten items in order, attach one item to each of the pegwords by means of a striking visual association. For example, to remember a 'to do' list that begins 'telephone mother, go to bank, buy newspaper' (in that order), you could associate 'telephoning mother' with the first pegword 'drum' (one) by imagining your mother banging a drum while on the phone to you, and the second pegword 'shoe' (two) with a mental image of your arrival at the bank and coins spilling from your shoes. The third item 'buy newspaper' could be associated with the third pegword 'knee' (three) using an image of you kneeling on an open newspaper. To recall the list of items to do, simply run through your original pegwords to be reminded of the images.

The same pegwords can be used time and again to remember different lists but be warned that your latest pegword list may replace your memory of older lists already stored, especially if they are not thoroughly learned or if they are listing similar items.

Narrative pegwords to remember numbers

The pegword system can be adapted for remembering digit sequences, for example, telephone numbers, PIN numbers and passwords. This time the images you create in your mind should form a short story in time so when you remember the story you remember the order of the digits. For example, to remember the bank card PIN number 2401, you might tell yourself the 'mini-story' of putting on a shoe (2) to kick open a burning door (4), revealing the Roman emperor Nero (0) banging a drum (1). You should also build in an image that tells you what the number is for – for example, the door on fire could be the door to the bank. The same applies for remembering telephone numbers – include in your story an image of the person whose number it is.

Number-shape system

You may find this system to remember numbers easier than the pegword number system just described. With this technique, the digits 0 to 9 are associated with images that are similar in shape to the digits themselves. It is best to think up your own images, but the following serve as an example:

> 0 an orange
> 1 a pen
> 2 a swan with a curved neck
> 3 an ear
> 4 a picnic table precariously balanced on one leg
> 5 a wheelchair or pushchair
> 6 a man with a large stomach
> 7 a walking stick
> 8 a woman
> 9 a giraffe (the stalk extended to form a long neck)

Like the rhyming pegwords, you need to commit your chosen images to memory. Once done, you can use them to remember any length of number by linking the images to form a 'story'. For example, to remember the number

24-906-5786 you might imagine a sequence of events as follows: a swan (2) lands on a picnic table, tipping it onto one leg (4), which upsets a giraffe (9) eating an orange (0), which drops onto the lap of a large man (6) seated in a pushchair (5), which then rolls down the slope over a walking stick (7) dropped by a woman (8); the man (6) shouts as he passes 'Sorry, can't stop!'. Notice how each image leads onto the next. Remember to make an association between the story and whatever the number represents. If it is a telephone number for Mr Rose, for example, you might envisage Mr Rose seated in the pushchair.

Link-word method

The link-word method is a variation on the peg system but instead of linking items to a well-learned structure it links the items to each other. The technique has been used extensively in the teaching of foreign languages and can also serve to extend native-language vocabulary, including the learning of technical terms, or for remembering difficult names. When using the system to learn foreign words, first associate the foreign word with an English word that sounds similar (the 'link word'), then link this word to the English meaning of the foreign word by means of an image. For example, the French for a stick of bread, 'la baguette', could be associated with two English words 'bag' and 'ate' that have a similar sound. These are the link words. The link words are then connected to the English meaning, 'French stick', by means of an image of a satisfied-looking 'bag' that just 'ate' a large French stick. For the method to be effective you must create your own images – they can be as strange as you like but must help you to visualize the link words and associate the meanings if they are to be useful.

Combining the pegword system with the link-word system

If you want to remember more than ten items, try combining the pegword system with the link-word system. Do this by associating the first item to be remembered with pegword 'thumb' (one), then link the next nine items together as you would in the link-word method. The eleventh item is then associated with pegword 'shoe' (two), and the following nine items are linked together. The twenty-first item is associated with pegword 'knee' (three), and so on. The pegwords act as cues for the item at the beginning of each link.

Face-name association

This visual mnemonic is useful for remembering faces and names. First select a distinctive feature of a face and associate the feature with a word or phrase that sounds like the person's name. Then create an image to link the feature to the name. For example, to remember someone called 'Philbee' who has a long chin, imagine the chin elongated to form a hook on which you hang a trilby hat ('trilby' rhymes with 'Philbee'). To recall his name, retrieve your image of the hook-like chin holding the trilby hat and you have a prompt for remembering 'Philbee'. You can use other information about people besides distinguishing physical features – their jobs, for example. Or you can make a visual association with someone you already know (or a well-known personality) who shares the same name by imagining them interacting in some way.

Verbal mnemonics

These techniques are particularly helpful if you prefer to use words instead of pictures to remember things.

Rhymes

Rhyme, rhythm and repetitive structure often make things easier to remember. For example, many of us use the rhyme 'In fourteen hundred and ninety-two, Columbus sailed the ocean blue' to remember the date Columbus discovered America. For spelling, we use the rhyme 'I before E except after C' to remember how to spell words like 'piece', 'niece' and 'deceive'. And for remembering the number of days in each month, the following is invaluable:

> Thirty days hath September,
> April, June and November,
> All the rest have thirty-one,
> Except February, which has twenty-eight,
> And in a leap year, twenty-nine

Try making up your own rhymes or rhyming words. For example, it might help to remember the first manned orbit of the moon using the rhyme 'Apollo VIII went round the moon in '68'.

Acrostics

Acrostics are first-letter mnemonics in which the initial letters of words in a sentence or verse correspond with those in the material that needs to be remembered, as in 'Richard Of York Gave Battle In Vain' for the colours of the rainbow (red, orange, yellow, green, blue, indigo, violet). Acrostics can be used to remember facts. For example, to remind yourself of the five kingdoms used to classify living organisms — Monerans, Protists, Fungi, Animals, Plants — you may use the sentence 'Many People Forget Animals and Plants'. Remember that acrostics give only the first letter as a prompt for remembering a word; you still need to learn the words themselves, usually by repetition.

Acronyms

Acronyms are common in both technical and ordinary language. They are words formed from the first letters of a series of words, for instance AIDS is an acronym from 'Acquired Immune Deficiency Syndrome' and 'radar' comes from 'radio detecting and ranging'. Acronyms can be used as a memory aid when the initial letters of a series of words form a meaningful word or name. For example, the word 'homes' can be used to remember the five great lakes, Huron, Ontario, Michigan, Erie and Superior. Try creating your own acronyms. Like acrostics, acronyms act as a prompt to remember information learnt by other means.

Number-to-code system

The number-to-code system, also known as the 'phonetic system', can be traced back to the seventeenth century and is one of the most powerful memory systems, but probably the most difficult to master. It can be used to remember long lists of items – far in excess of ten or twenty objects – and is also helpful for remembering long numbers, appointments, historical dates, playing cards, birthdays, economic data and many other things.

The system turns numbers into phonetic codes, which are in turn translated into codewords. The codewords are more memorable than numbers because they are meaningful.

At the heart of the system are the following phonetic codes for numbers 0 to 9:

Number	Code	To help you remember
0	z, s, soft c	'z' is the first letter of the word 'zero'
1	t, th, d	't' has one downstroke
2	n	'n' has two downstrokes
3	m	'm' has three downstrokes
4	r	'r' is the last letter in the word 'four'

5	l	'l' is the Roman numeral for 50 (a multiple of five)
6	j, sh, soft ch, soft g	'j' written by hand looks like 6 in mirror image
7	k, q, hard c, hard g, ng	'k' is the first letter of film-maker's name Kurosawa who directed *Seven Samurai*
8	f, v	'f' is the first letter of film-maker's name Fellini who directed the film *8 1/2*
9	p, b	'p' written by hand looks like 9 (nine) in mirror image

NB: Vowels are not coded in this system; nor are the consonants 'w', 'h' and 'y'.

First learn this list of codes. Then for numbers 1 to 10 (or 1 to 100, or 1 to 1000, depending on how extensive you want to make your system) use these codes to create a codeword and an associated image for each digit. For example, for number 1, create a codeword that begins with either 't', 'th' or 'd', which could be 'tea', 'tie', 'day' or 'toe' (a codeword must not include codes relating to any other number), and an associated image (for example, a cup of tea). For number 19 you could use codewords 'tip', 'tub', 'dub' or 'dip'. For number 128 you could use 'tin of' (a codeword can be in two parts). Lists of codewords for numbers 1 to 100 or 1 to

1000 are provided in some memory training books – refer to these if you don't want to make up your own. Once you have a list of codewords and associated images, you must commit them to memory. You are then ready to use the system for memorizing material.

To use the system for remembering a long number, for example, 3520981749, there are several options depending on how many numbers you have memorized as codewords. If you know codewords for numbers 1 to 100, you can 'chunk' the digits into groups of twos (35-20-98-17-49), which translate into codewords 'mile' (35), 'nose' (20), 'beef' (98), 'duck' (17) and 'rope' (49). Then remember these words by creating a memorable sentence or story linking them in sequence. For example, imagine yourself walking a mile (35), following your nose (20), to find a joint of beef (98) and a roast duck (17). If you have codewords for numbers 1 to 10, then the digits 3520981749 translate individually into 'm-l-n-s-b-f-t-k-r-b'. To remember this code, use an acrostic (a memorable sentence), such as 'Melanie loves neon stockings bought from trendy Kensington retail boutiques'.

The number-to-code system is very versatile. For example, to remember a dental appointment at 8 am on 14 September (14/9), translate the time and date into codewords and use the codewords to form a memorable image, story or acrostic that will help you recall the appointment. The time (8) translates into codeword 'off'; the date (14/9) translates into 'door' and 'paw'; your memorable image might involve you falling 'off' your seat when the dentist's 'door' opens revealing a large 'paw'.

You can apply the system to remembering birthdays or historical dates. For example, 1789, the beginning of the French Revolution, gives codes t–k–f–b for each digit in the date, which can be used to make the memorable sentence 'The King Falls Badly'.

To use it to remember playing cards takes a little more effort. Following the practice of some memory experts, you apply a special codeword to each card in the pack. The special codeword begins with the first letter of the suit of the card and ends with the code representing the number of the card. For example, the five of diamonds receives the codeword 'doll'. You then memorize special codewords for all fifty-two cards, together with an image for each codeword, and practise recalling the images whenever the associated cards come up. If you are a regular card player, the system can be highly effective. For example, when playing bridge or other card games, there is a distinct advantage in knowing which cards are waiting to be played. With the number-to-code system you can quickly assess which cards have been played – and, by deduction, which have not – because as soon as a card is shown, you instantly recall its associated image. Those cards waiting to be played are recognizable by the absence of their associated images in your mind. It is also a distinct advantage in many card games to remember which cards are held by other players, and the number-to-code system can help with this too. For example, if you deduce that Peter is holding the five of diamonds, by making a visual association between Peter and the codeword for this card ('doll') you rapidly fix this information in memory. Of course, the system requires many hours of practice and you may prefer instead to improve your level of card playing by developing your concentration and working memory.

Final note

This chapter has introduced a range of strategies for memory improvement. These all require practice. Use the memory tests in chapter five to practise memory techniques and find out which systems work best for you.

5

TESTING YOUR MEMORY

How to use the tests

This chapter provides tests to assess six areas of memory:
Test 1: Social/adaptive memory (names and faces, birthdays and anniversaries, appointments)
Test 2: Visual-spatial memory (scene, abstract drawing, mental rotation, spatial orientation)
Test 3: Working memory (playing cards, word pairs, reading)
Test 4: Factual memory (facts, definitions)
Test 5: Numerical memory (digit span, mental calculation)
Test 6: Verbal and auditory memory (word manipulation, word lists, heard story)

Use the tests to assess and develop memory functioning in each area. You can either turn directly to those tests that exercise your weakest areas of memory functioning, or work through all the tests.

After each test check your performance against the indicator and follow the suggestions for improving your score. Note that memory performance depends on individual interests and experiences and there is no single objective scale against which to measure the effectiveness of your memory. The tests provided here cannot give definitive results but they can be used to give an indication of your memory's efficiency.

Begin tests

Test 1: Social/adaptive memory

Social/adaptive memory stores information learned from interactions in social settings. It involves the ability to acquire, access and use information in order to meet social or community expectations, for example, to memorize and recall a person's name at a party, or to remember how to behave at a particular social event.

If you have a good social/adaptive memory you have no difficulty relating to people, learning from them and behaving appropriately in their company. You are adept at remembering faces and names, birthdays and anniversaries, family conventions and social rules belonging to your culture. You adapt easily to different surroundings and cope well with the responsibilities of everyday life, including daily organization, time-keeping and attendance at appointments. People can turn to you for support and you probably are a good listener and remember much of what is said to you.

Social/adaptive memory is vital for good relations with other people. Improving your social and adaptive memory will strengthen your organizational skills and relationships, and help you to consider other people's points of view.

The social/adaptive memory tests in this book are designed to exercise your social/adaptive memory. They are not given under controlled conditions, nor have they been subjected to rigorous standardization and normalization so they cannot provide definitive results. The score you achieve is merely meant to be an indicator of how you might perform in a professional and scientifically controlled test of social/adaptive memory ability. In short, the results should only be interpreted as a broad estimate of this ability.

At the end of each test there are hints on how to improve your performance.

1.1 Names and faces

This is a test of social/adaptive memory in which you memorize faces and names. An ability to remember names and faces is a great asset in social and business contexts.

Look at the eight pictures below and memorize the names. Notice the facial characteristics and use them to help you remember each name. You have two minutes, then turn the page and answer the questions.

Sally Thomas   Owain Jones   Abdul Ramadan

Robert Lauper   Esme Chaplin   John Adams

Sylvia Coot   Humphrey Waters

Write down the name of each person.

How did you do?

Number of faces and names recalled (out of 8):

0–2	*3–6*	*More than 6*
→ Below average	→ Average	→ Above average

How to improve your performance

Tips for improving attention are on pages 100–2. Techniques for remembering names and faces are on pages 104, 122 and 123–4. Try making associations between the names and people you already know or who are in the media (for example, someone called Esme Chaplin could be associated with Charlie Chaplin). Alternatively, focus on something each person reminds you of.

1.2 Birthdays and anniversaries

This is a test of social/adaptive memory in which you memorize the birthdays and anniversaries of some of your friends and relatives.

On the page opposite, write down four birthdays and four anniversaries that you haven't memorized in the past. Take three minutes to learn all the dates. Then turn the page.

Birthdays

Name   Date

----------------------------   --------------------------

----------------------------   --------------------------

----------------------------   --------------------------

----------------------------   --------------------------

Anniversaries

Name   Date

----------------------------   --------------------------

----------------------------   --------------------------

----------------------------   --------------------------

----------------------------   --------------------------

Write down the names and dates below, then test yourself again after five hours:

Name	Date
-------------------------	-------------------------
-------------------------	-------------------------
-------------------------	-------------------------
-------------------------	-------------------------
-------------------------	-------------------------
-------------------------	-------------------------
-------------------------	-------------------------
-------------------------	-------------------------

How did you do?

Number of dates recalled immediately (out of 8):

0–2	*3–6*	*More than 6*
➜ Below average	➜ Average	➜ Above average

How to improve your results

Whether you maintain your score after five hours will depend on your technique for remembering dates and the number of times you rehearse them. Each time you recall the dates, the rate of forgetting is reduced. Turn to pages 112–13 for information about repetition in learning, and pages 118–22 for techniques for remembering dates. Get into the habit of sending birthday and anniversary cards each month. Use a diary to check your recall.

1.3 Appointments

This is a test of your ability to recall plans for the week ahead. Remembering appointments and other dates shows you are able to think about life in an organized way and you have a positive attitude towards meeting social obligations.

Look closely at this page from a diary. Take three minutes to memorize the information, then turn the page.

JANUARY

9 **Monday**

10 am   *Dentist*   7 pm   *National Theatre*

10 **Tuesday**

1 pm   *Lunch with Gregor*   3 pm   *Meeting with editor*

11 **Wednesday**

9.30 am   *Phone Winston*

12 **Thursday**

8.30 am   *School drop*   1 pm   *Lunch meeting re new book*

13 **Friday**

8.30 am   *School drop*   8.30 pm   *Penny and Steven for dinner*

14 **Saturday**

Take children swimming   2.30 pm   *Meet Sandra in town*

15 **Sunday**

Lunch at Hattie's

Try and recall the diary entries below:

Monday

Tuesday

Wednesday

Thursday

Friday

Saturday

Sunday

How did you do?
Number of entries recalled (out of 12):

0–2	*3–7*	*More than 7*
➜ Below average	➜ Average	➜ Above average

How to improve your performance
Turn to pages 102–4 for tips on bringing organization into your life and pages 126–30 for the number-to-code system, which can be used to remember appointments. The method of loci (116–18) and the pegword systems (118–20) can also be adapted for remembering diary events. Always use a diary as a back-up.

Test 2: Visual–spatial memory

Visual-spatial memory involves remembering pictures and images in particular. It involves the ability to take in information presented visually, especially in three-dimensional space, to process and manipulate that information in working (short-term) memory, and to store and retrieve it from long-term memory.

People with good visual-spatial memory have no difficulty noticing details and visualizing objects and places, and are often better at remembering things they have read than things they have heard or been told. Usually they are good at drawing from memory, probably good at judging the speed of an oncoming car or comparing the shapes and visual characteristics of things, and good at performing various spatial manipulation tasks, like rotating three-dimensional objects in their mind, or reading a map. They probably have a strong imagination. Good visual-spatial memory is recognized to be a contributing factor to success in careers such as architecture, mathematics, engineering and other technology-associated functions. There is some evidence that males on average score better in visual-spatial tests than females, which may account for the high proportion of men engaged in careers such as these.

The ability to visualize objects and manipulate them in working memory is a vital aspect of a person's capabilities. Without it, the simple act of remembering how to move from your kitchen to your bathroom would be impossibly difficult. Improving visual-spatial abilities is helpful for memory: you will find it easier to interpret and store visual information and you will be more successful at applying mnemonic systems, many of which rely on visualizations.

The visual-spatial tests in this book are designed to exercise both short-term (working) and long-term visual-spatial memory. They are not given under controlled conditions, nor have they been subjected to rigorous standardization and normalization, so they cannot provide definitive results. The score you achieve is merely meant to be an indicator of how you might perform in a professional and scientifically controlled test of visual-spatial memory ability. In short, the results should only be interpreted as a broad estimate of this ability.

At the end of each test there are hints on how to improve your performance.

2.1 Scene

This is a test of visual–spatial memory. Study the picture below for two minutes. Then turn the page and answer the questions.

1   The bus is outside which two shops?
2   What is advertised on the bus?
3   How many flags are in the scene?
4   What is happening opposite the bus stop?
5   Who is waiting at the bus stop?
6   What time is it?
7   In which direction are the pedal bikes heading?
8   When is the next cinema showing?
9   How many children are playing in the playground?
10 In which direction are the jogger and rollerskater heading?

Answers

1: Chemist and butcher; 2: News Weekly; 3: 5;
4: Roadworks; 5: A man, a woman and a child; 6: 4.20 pm;
7: Away from the shopping mall; 8: 6.50 pm; 9: 6;
10: Towards the shopping mall

How did you do?

Number of questions answered correctly (out of 10):

0–2	3–6	More than 6
→ Below average	→ Average	→ Above average

How to improve your performance

Try applying the method of chunking (see page 108) to interpret and remember the picture. This involves grouping together different elements of the scene to make sense of them and remember them in relation to other groups or objects in the scene. For example, the first 'chunk' could be the area around the bus – repeat to yourself (and see in your mind's eye) the number 61 bus, travelling in the direction of the shopping mall (in the opposite direction to the fruit van and two bicycles) and stopping outside the butcher and chemist shops. A man, woman and child are waiting at the stop, and there are roadworks opposite. It may help to form a story in your head of what is happening – repeating it to yourself helps lodge it in auditory memory. When you have analyzed and formed mental images of each chunk of the scene, try and visualize the whole picture. Turn away from the picture several times and return to it, checking and correcting the mental image you have stored. This image of the overall scene will act as a prompt when you come to recall the details. See pages 100–2 for hints on improving concentration, and page 110 for more about visualization.

2.2 Abstract drawing

This is a test of perceptual organization and visual memory. Study the abstract drawing below for two minutes. Draw it on the page opposite if it helps to lodge it in memory. Then turn over the page and recreate the drawing from memory.

Practise the drawing here.

Recreate the drawing from memory here.

How did you do?

Compare your drawing with the original and check the following:

	Yes	No
1 Did you remember the main structure of the figure (the overall shape and main intersecting lines)?		
2 Did you remember more than 50% of the incidental (non-structural) elements?		
3 Did you remember less than 50% of the incidental (non-structural) elements?		

You answered 'no' to questions 1 and 2, and 'yes' to question 3.
→ Below average

You answered 'yes' to questions 1 and 3 and 'no' to question 2. You show a good memory for the structure and organization of visual information. You probably interpreted the structure in terms of an object it reminded you of, for example, a boat, which helped you to recall the overall shape.
→ Average

You answered 'yes' to questions 1 and 2.
→ Above average

How to improve your performance

Abstract drawings are the most difficult to remember. Try relating the shape to something meaningful, that it reminds you of. Once you can memorize the main structure, then practise filling in the details, again by relating them to more meaningful objects and shapes, or by holding an image in your head of the pattern created by the abstract elements and returning to it repeatedly. The act of drawing and redrawing the picture will help you to remember it. It also helps if you are practised at drawing. Tips for improving concentration are on pages 100–2.

2.3 Mental rotation

This tests your ability to imagine how something appears from another perspective, a useful skill for orientating yourself and map-reading. It requires you to hold and manipulate visual information in working memory.

Look closely at the cluster of cubes marked A. Then mentally rotate each cube cluster B–E and decide which if any are the same as cube cluster A. There is a time limit of three minutes.

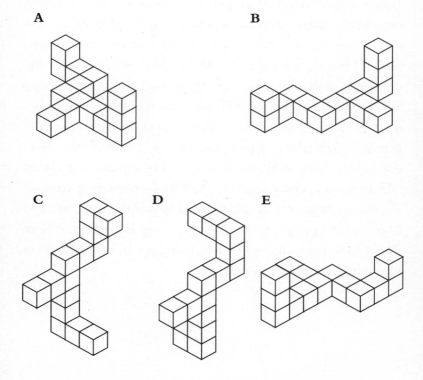

Answers

Cubes C and E are the same as the cube cluster A.

How did you do?

Number of matching cube clusters identified (out of 2):

Zero	*One*	*Two*
→ Below average	→ Average	→ Above average

How to improve your performance

When inspecting cube cluster A, imagine yourself standing next to the three cubes at the end of the cluster, and analyse the sequence from this point. Then for each cube cluster, find the same three cubes, 'stand' beside them and rotate the cluster in your mind so you 'see' it from the same angle as cluster 'A'. If you find it difficult to manipulate visual information in this way, you probably find map-reading and drawing particularly challenging. Get into the habit of viewing objects from different angles. Taking up drawing classes will help your observation skills. When orientating yourself in a new environment, take time to notice the structure and layout of the place you are in, which way is north, and how things look from all perspectives. See page 103 for advice on improving awareness in new places.

2.4 Spatial orientation

This is a test of your ability to orientate yourself in three-dimensional space, in particular your ability to imagine yourself in an environment based on information provided by a plan or a map. It requires you to hold and manipulate a mental picture in working memory.

Memorize the department store floor plans on the next page. After two minutes turn the page and answer the questions.

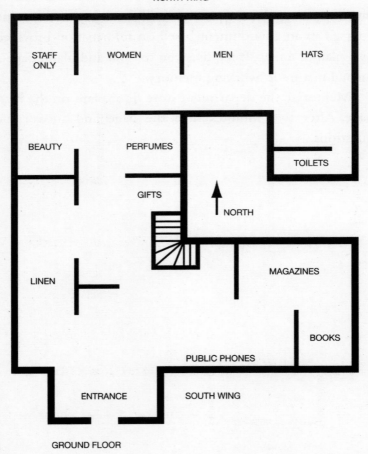

NORTH WING

STAFF ONLY   WOMEN   MEN   HATS

BEAUTY   PERFUMES   TOILETS

GIFTS

NORTH

LINEN   MAGAZINES

BOOKS

PUBLIC PHONES

ENTRANCE   SOUTH WING

GROUND FLOOR

NORTH WING

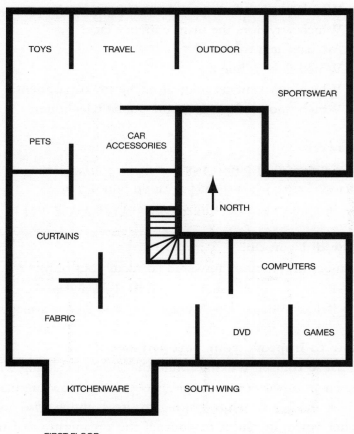

TOYS

TRAVEL

OUTDOOR

SPORTSWEAR

PETS

CAR
ACCESSORIES

NORTH

CURTAINS

COMPUTERS

FABRIC

DVD

GAMES

KITCHENWARE

SOUTH WING

FIRST FLOOR

1   Are perfumes on the first floor?
2   Are the toilets on the ground floor?
3   Which floor and wing is kitchenware?
4   Which way does the main entrance face?
5   Are hats next to men's?
6   Which floor is linen?
7   Which departments are near to the toy department?
8   Which floor and wing are the public telephones?

Answers

8: Ground floor, south wing
6: Ground floor; 7: Pets, Travel, Car accessories;
1: No; 2: Yes; 3: First floor, south wing; 4: South; 5: Yes;

How did you do?

Number of questions answered correctly (out of 8):

| *0–2* | *3–6* | *More than 6* |
| → Below average | → Average | → Above average |

How to improve your performance

Visualize yourself walking round the shop, interacting with the environment. For example, 'see' yourself browsing magazines and books while waiting to use a phone. Use your 'inner voice' to repeat to yourself the organization of the shop, for example, beauty and perfumes are opposite each other, phones are near the entrance. When visiting new places make a point of using plans or maps. See page 103 for advice on improving awareness in a new environment.

Test 3: Working memory

Your working (or 'short-term') memory is crucial for remembering a telephone number long enough to dial it, for understanding the meaning of a sentence, or for calculating a sum in your head. It is what you are currently holding in your conscious mind at any point in time and is one of the most important concepts in understanding and improving your memory. The role of working memory in the memory process is explained in chapter three.

If you have a good working memory you will be adept at holding information in your head while you 'inspect' or analyse it, for example, while working out your next chess move. You will probably be a good card player, as you can decide which card to play while keeping track of who holds what. You may also be good at multi-tasking because of your ability to transfer your attention from one thing to another and back again without forgetting what you were doing. People who have difficulty concentrating, who forget what they were doing or why they went into a room, or who are easily distracted could benefit from trying to improve their working memory.

Working memory capacity is limited to those items that you are actively thinking about at any one moment in time. It is possible to improve the processing power of working memory and slightly increase its capacity to retain information in consciousness. Improvements are usually made by learning to concentrate for longer periods and using techniques to organize the information you take in from outside.

The working memory tests in this book are designed to exercise your working memory. They are not given under controlled conditions, nor have they been subjected to rigorous standardization and normalization, so they cannot provide definitive results. The score you achieve is merely meant to be an indicator of how you might perform in a professional and scientifically controlled test of working memory. In short, the results should only be interpreted as a broad estimate of this ability.

At the end of each test there are hints on how to improve your scores.

3.1 Playing cards

This test involves holding playing cards in working memory. You have two minutes to memorize who has which cards. Then turn the page.

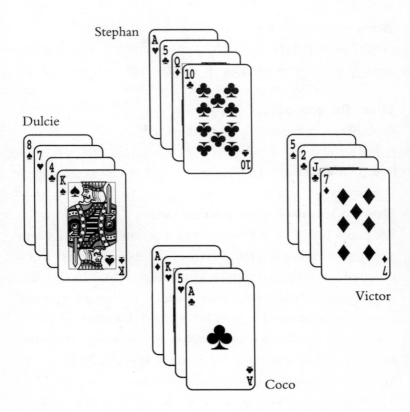

1   Who holds the ace of hearts?
2   Who holds the queen of diamonds?
3   Who holds the ace of clubs?
4   Who holds the jack of clubs?
5   Who holds the king of spades?
6   Who holds the four of clubs?

Answers

5: Dulcie; 6: Dulcie

1: Stephan; 2: Stephan; 3: Coco; 4: Victor;

How did you do?

Number of questions answered correctly:

0–2	3–4	More than 4
→ Below average	→ Average	→ Above average

How to improve your performance

See pages 100–2 for hints on improving concentration. Cards are more meaningful, and therefore more memorable, when grouped into suits and into numbers high to low. Notice first the highest valued card of each hand and create a visual association to remember who holds them (for example, Coco has the ace of diamonds – imagine her expensive diamond necklace). Then relate the other cards of each hand to the high cards (try using the narrative story method on page 118). The number-to-code system on pages 126–30 can be used to remember playing cards.

3.2 Word pairs

This test involves memorizing pairs of words in a short period of time, then using one word of each pair to prompt the recall of its paired associate.

You have sixty seconds to memorize the word pairs below, then turn the page.

1	Story	Celebration
2	Prospect	Number
3	Cook	Balkans
4	Dimension	Collide
5	Price	Tournament
6	Insurgent	Psychiatry
7	Forthcoming	Sustainable
8	Extremism	Lonely
9	Spill	Bright
10	Storm	Generate

Write down the paired word for each of the following:

1 Story   ------------------------------------
2 Prospect   ------------------------------------
3 Cook   ------------------------------------
4 Dimension   ------------------------------------
5 Price   ------------------------------------
6 Insurgent   ------------------------------------
7 Forthcoming ------------------------------------
8 Extremism   ------------------------------------
9 Spill   ------------------------------------
10 Storm   ------------------------------------

How did you do?

Number of paired words recalled (out of 10):

| *0–5* | *6–9* | *All 10* |
| ➡ Below average | ➡ Average | ➡ Above average |

How to improve your performance

Learning items in associated pairs allows you to hold more in memory than learning them individually. This is because recall of one item prompts the recall of its pair. As you read each word, visualize the object it represents and imagine it interacting with the object represented by the paired associate. For example, imagine someone you know telling a story about a particular celebration. Return to these images when you want to recall the words. Abstract concepts are more difficult to visualize than concrete objects, and some-times a memorable phrase or sentence involving both paired words is more helpful than a visualization. Repeat the phrase or sentence to yourself to lodge it in auditory memory. See page 110 for information on forming visualizations and associations. Special techniques for remembering lists of items are on pages 116–20.

3.3 Reading memory

This tests your ability to register and grasp the meaning of information presented in reading matter. The test requires efficient use of working memory and good concentration.

Read through the passage slowly. As soon as you have finished reading, answer the questions without looking back at the text. You have six minutes to complete the whole test.

Extract from *Mosaïque* by Prosper Mérimée (1833):

The bull–ring at Madrid can hold about seven thousand spectators, who go in and out with no confusion by a large number of gates. You sit down on benches of wood or stone; a few boxes contain chairs. His Catholic Majesty's is the only one that is fairly elegantly decorated.

The arena is surrounded by a strong palisade, about five-and-a-half feet in height. Two feet from the ground, all around and on both sides of the palisade, extends a wooden ledge, a sort of causeway which helps the pursued toreador to jump the more easily over the barrier, and is moreover protected by a double rope fastened by strong stakes. It is a fairly recent precaution. A bull had not only jumped the barrier, which happens often, but had even flung himself on the tiers, where he had killed or maimed dozens of sightseers. The tight rope is thought to prevent the recurrence of a similar accident.

Four doors open on to the arena. One communicates with the bulls' stable; another leads to the butcher, where the bulls are flayed and dissected. The two others are for the human actors in this tragedy...

The bull-ring looks very animated. The arena, well before the combat, is full of people, and the tiers and boxes provide a confused mass of heads. There are two kinds of seats: the ones in the shade are most expensive and the most comfortable, but the sunny side is always provided with intrepid amateurs. You see many fewer women than men and most of them are of the manola class. However, in the boxes you can observe some elegant outfits, though few young women. The Spaniards have recently been perverted by French and English novels, and have removed their respect for their ancient costume. I do not think that ecclesiastics are forbidden to attend these spectacles: however I never saw but one in costume. I have been told that several go there in disguise.

At a signal given by the president of the fight, an alguazil major, accompanied by two alguazils in short cloaks, all three on horseback, and followed by a company of cavalry, evacuate the arena and the narrow corridor that separates it from the tiers. When they and their retinue have returned, a herald, escorted by a lawyer and more alguazils on foot, comes to the centre of the ring to read out a ban that forbids anyone to throw anything into the arena, or to disturb the combatants with cries or signals, etc. Hardly has he appeared when, in spite of the respectable formula: 'In the house of the King, our lord, whom God preserve', whooping and whistling arises on all sides, and lasts the whole time of the reading of the rules, which in any case are never observed. In the ring, and only there, the people command the sovereign, and can say and do just as they please…

One of the mounted alguazils receives a key in his hat, which is thrown to him by the president of the games. This key opens nothing; but nevertheless he takes it to the man responsible for opening the bulls' stable, and makes off straightaway at full gallop, accompanied by hoots from the multitude, who shout that the bull is already loose and behind him. This witticism is repeated at every fight.

Meanwhile the picadors have taken up their positions. Normally there are two mounted ones in the arena; two or three others stay outside, ready to replace them in case of accidents such as death, severe fracture, etc…

The bull, preferably expressly provoked while in his cage, rushes furiously out. Usually he reaches the middle of the plaza, in one dash, and there stops, astonished by the noise he hears and by the spectators all round him. On his neck he carries a little knot of ribbons attached by a little hook stuck in the flesh. The colour of these ribbons shows what herd he is from; but a skilled amateur can tell at a single sight of the animal, what province and what race he is from.

Now answer the questions opposite.

1 How many spectators can the bull-ring hold?
2 For whom is the elegantly decorated chair intended?
3 For what purpose is the wooden ledge on both sides of the palisade?
4 Which seats are the most expensive?
5 What does the herald read out in the centre of the arena?
6 Who throws a key to a mounted alguazil?
7 How many mounted picadors are there normally in the arena?
8 What does the colour of the ribbons on the bull's neck indicate?

Answers

1: 7,000; 2: The king; 3: So the toreador can jump easily over the barrier and escape the bull; 4: The seats in the shade; 5: A ban that forbids anyone to throw anything into the arena, or to disturb the combatants; 6: The president; 7: Two; 8: The herd the bull is from

How did you do?

Number of questions answered correctly (out of 8):

| 0–2 | 3–5 | More than 5 |
| → Below average | → Average | → Above average |

How to improve your performance

See pages 100–2 for advice on improving concentration, which will help you take in what you are reading and hold it in working memory long enough to make sense of it. As you read the passage, visualize what is being described. Try and 'see' things moving, their shapes and colours, 'feel' the textures and the heat of the sun, and 'hear' the crowd and other sounds. The more detail you can build into your mental image, the stronger the impression in memory and the longer you will have access to it. Read the passage again and practise visualizing the scene. It takes longer to read this way but the improvement in attention and memory more than compensate. There is more about visualization on page 110.

Test 4: Factual memory

Factual memory stores knowledge about the world (historical, geographical, scientific and cultural facts) and sensory knowledge (such as knowing the smell of the sea or the taste of butter). We manipulate and process factual information in working (short-term) memory for storage in long-term memory.

Most educationalists now accept that acquiring conceptual understanding and cognitive skills is more important than memorizing a library of factual information (Williams & Burden, 1997). However, a good factual memory is still considered essential if we are to study effectively and pass examinations, and many people find that efficient factual storage and retrieval is helpful in both professional and social life.

Learning facts traditionally involved rote repetition of material. In current thinking, blind repetition does not help understanding or genuine learning and must be practised along with other learning techniques. For example, Lewis (1986) identifies an effective method for absorbing information in exploring and becoming thoroughly interested in a subject.

Accessing facts stored in long-term memory can prove problematic. Many people have experienced the 'tip-of-the tongue' phenomenon, in which they feel they know the information but cannot retrieve it when needed. Methods to help retrieve information from long-term memory are described on pages 113–15.

The factual memory tests in this book are designed to exercise your semantic memory, which stores knowledge about the world. They are not given under controlled conditions, nor have they been subjected to rigorous standardization and normalization so they cannot provide definitive results. The score you achieve is merely meant to be an indicator of how you might perform in a professional and scientifically controlled test of factual memory ability. In short, the results should only be interpreted as a broad estimate of this ability.

At the end of each test there are hints on how to improve your performance.

4.1 Recall of facts

This test involves recalling from long-term memory several well-known facts. As each person's knowledge reflects their personal interests, age, culture and experience, a more accurate indication of your ability to access factual memory is gained when questions are chosen to reflect your particular interests and learning experience. The second part of the test is designed with this in mind.

You have sixty seconds to write down your answers to the following questions (the answers are on the next page):

1 What are the dates of the Second World War?
2 When was the first Gulf War?
3 What is the capital of Zimbabwe?
4 What is the capital of The Netherlands?
5 Who wrote the ballets *The Nutcracker, Swan Lake* and *The Sleeping Beauty*?
6 Who directed the films *Battleship Potemkin* and *Ivan the Terrible*?
7 In Greek legend, who is the god of all gods and god of light and weather?
8 Who invented the light bulb in 1879?
9 Which political leader was in charge of the Soviet Union during the Second World War?
10 Name the Indian nationalist leader and social reformer who was assassinated in 1948.

Answers

8: Thomas Edison; **9:** Joseph Stalin; **10:** Mahatma Gandhi
5: Tchaikovsky; **6:** Sergei Eisenstein; **7:** Zeus;
1: 1939–45; **2:** 1991; **3:** Harare; **4:** Amsterdam;

How did you do?

Number of facts recalled (out of 10):

0–2	*3–6*	*More than 6*
➜ Below average	➜ Average	➜ Above average

Now look up ten facts you do not already know and learn them at your own pace. Use the spaces below to record a question that will test your recall of each fact. Check your ability to recall at the following intervals: immediately after learning, one hour after learning, one week after learning, and at increasingly longer intervals.

1 ---

2 ---

3 ---

4 ---

5 ---

6 ---

7 ---

8 ---

9 ---

10 ---

How to improve your performance

Your score will depend on how recently you learnt the facts and how regularly you have recalled them correctly. For example, something learnt over five years ago but recalled only once since first learning is unlikely to be retrieved from memory without prompting. When memorizing new material, the likelihood of it being lodged in long-term memory is dramatically increased if you keep testing yourself. See pages 112–13 for the method of 'expanded rehearsal'. Pages 113–15 give tips for retrieving information from long-term memory, which can be useful if you experience the 'tip-of-the tongue' phenomenon. See pages 107–13 for general advice on learning, and pages 115–30 for mnemonic techniques for storing facts.

4.2 Definitions

This tests your ability to process verbal information in working memory and recall target words from long-term memory.

Read the definitions and produce the target words as quickly as possible (the answers are on the following page). You have sixty seconds to complete the test.

Definition   Target word

1   The leaves of a plant or tree.   ------------------
2   A small copy or imitation of an
existing object, often made to scale.   ------------------
3   The act of offering the life of a
person or animal in homage to a deity.   ------------------
4   A device for separating solid
particles or impurities from a liquid by
passing it through a porous substance.   ------------------
5   A head harness for guiding a horse,
consisting of headstall, bit and reins.   ------------------
6   A recess or hollow in a wall, often
used to place a statue, bust or vase.   ------------------
7   The vacation spent together by a
newly married couple.   ------------------
8   A gathering of people for religious
worship or teaching.   ------------------

9 A system of medical treatment based on the theory that some diseases can be cured by giving small doses of drugs which in a healthy person would produce symptoms like those of the disease. ------------------

10 A sign or warning of a future event; an omen. ------------------

Answers

1: Foliage; 2: Model; 3: Sacrifice; 4: Filter; 5: Bridle; 6: Niche; 7: Honeymoon; 8: Congregation; 9: Homeopathy; 10: Presage

How did you do?

Number of correct target words (out of 10):

0–2	*3–7*	*More than 7*
→ Below average	→ Average	→ Above average

How to improve your performance

Your score will depend on your personal interests, language skills and experience. If English is not your first language you may find this test particularly difficult. Tips for retrieving information from long-term memory are on pages 113–15. Try these techniques especially if you experience the 'tip-of-the tongue' phenomenon. General tips for learning are on pages 107–13. A mnemonic technique for extending vocabulary (the link-word method) is on pages 122–3.

Test 5: Numerical memory

Numerical memory stores information presented in numerical form rather than in words or pictures. This includes telephone numbers, pin numbers, numerical codes, statistical
information, economic data, mathematical formulae, meas-
urements, sports results, and so on.

The ability to remember and use numerical information
is a vital aspect of a person's capabilities. Without it, the simple act of holding a number in your mind long enough to
make a simple calculation, or a telephone number before
you dial it would be almost impossible. Experimental work
carried out by J. Jacobs in 1887 introduced the concept of
'digit span' to measure the capacity to hold numerical data
in working (short-term) memory. This concept is influential
in psychology to this day and is a feature of the first test in
this section.

A person who has a good numerical memory is usually
adept at holding and manipulating numbers in conscious
(working) memory. Good numerical memory is undoubtedly an asset in careers such as mathematics, engineering and
computing.

Many people find numbers difficult to remember
because they are abstract and not concrete. Memory techniques address this problem by relating numbers to words or
pictures, which add meaning and make the numbers easier
to recall. Simply grouping or 'chunking' numbers together
can also help us to remember them, for example, telephone

numbers are often represented in international and local codes. A number represented as 020-8741-3663 (instead of 02087413663) is easier to hold in working memory than eleven individual digits.

The numerical memory tests in this book are designed to exercise your short-term and long-term numerical memory. They are not given under controlled conditions, nor have they been subjected to rigorous standardization and normalization, so they cannot provide definitive results. The score you achieve is merely meant to be an indicator of how you might perform in a professional and scientifically controlled test of numerical memory ability. In short, the results should only be interpreted as a broad estimate of this ability.

At the end of each test there are hints on how to improve your performance.

5.1 Digit span

This test, based on experimental work by Jacobs (1887), is designed to measure the capacity of your short-term (working) numerical memory.

Read aloud the numbers below, beginning with the smallest. After each number, cover the page and try to remember the digits in the correct order (write them down to check). If you recall the digits correctly, move on to the next number. Continue until you find a number length that you always get wrong. This will determine the number of digits you can hold in working memory – your digit span.

5982		93702	
3049	→	30581	→
4810		04592	
5603		87412	

	859247		0498120	
→	301972	→	5938293	→
	384038		9401958	
	940698		5497813	

	82941329		948603928	
→	48750298	→	394860193	↗
	39587374		403968369	
	05938273		940285916	

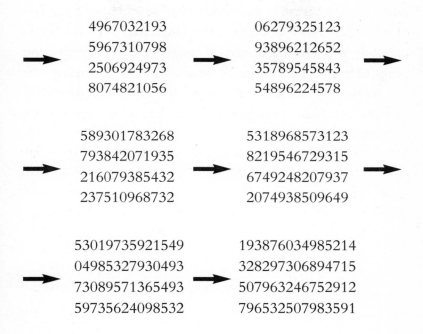

4967032193
5967310798
2506924973
8074821056

06279325123
93896212652
35789545843
54896224578

589301783268
793842071935
216079385432
237510968732

5318968573123
8219546729315
6749248207937
2074938509649

53019735921549
04985327930493
73089571365493
59735624098532

193876034985214
328297306894715
507963246752912
796532507983591

How did you do?

Digit span:

| 4–5 digits | 6–9 digits | *More than 9 digits* |
| → Below average | → Average | → Above average |

How to improve your results

When reading the number sequences aloud, group the digits rhythmically in chunks of threes, or threes and twos. Concentrate on the sound and rhythm of the numbers. It may help to visualize the numbers as written. See page 108 for further information on 'chunking', page 110 for information on visualization, and pages 101–2 for tips on improving concentration. Mnemonic techniques for remembering numbers are on pages 120–2 (narrative peg-words and number-shape system) and 126–30 (number-to-code system).

5.2 Mental calculation

This is a test of your concentration and ability to manipulate numbers in working memory.

Follow the route below, making the required calculations along the way. Do not write anything down. Allow yourself three minutes to complete the test.

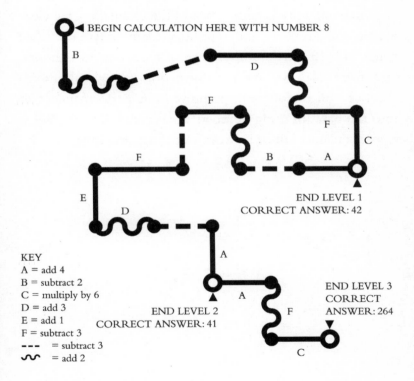

BEGIN CALCULATION HERE WITH NUMBER 8

B

D

F

F

C

F

B A

END LEVEL 1
CORRECT ANSWER: 42

E

D

A

END LEVEL 3
CORRECT
ANSWER: 264

END LEVEL 2
CORRECT ANSWER: 41

F

C

KEY
A = add 4
B = subtract 2
C = multiply by 6
D = add 3
E = add 1
F = subtract 3
--- = subtract 3
∿ = add 2

How did you do?

| *Calculation error* *during level 1* → Below average | *Calculation error* *during level 2* → Average | *Calculation correct* *up to level 3* → Above average |

How to improve your performance

Turn to pages 100–2 for tips on improving concentration. If you have difficulty keeping track of the calculation, try visualizing the numbers and repeating them to yourself (see pages 112–13 for the importance of repetition to memory, and page 110 for more information on visualization). Practice will undoubtedly improve your performance. Get into the habit of using numbers in everyday life, whether it is to calculate a bill or to work out a cooking time.

Test 6: Verbal and auditory memory

Verbal and auditory memory involves an ability to remember information presented verbally (using words), especially heard information. It involves taking in, processing and manipulating verbal and heard information in working (short-term) memory, and storing and retrieving it from long-term memory. Repeating words to ourselves in working memory is an important function in verbal and auditory memory. In the Baddeley and Hitch model of working memory (1974), the 'inner voice' element of working memory allows us to rehearse and 'hear' words in our heads, and is important for learning a language, including normal language development in our own first language.

Verbal and auditory memory is vital for functioning in society. For example, without the ability to understand and remember words, communication would be impossible. People with good verbal and auditory memory are often skilled in remembering things they are told. They probably have an extensive vocabulary, enjoy crossword puzzles and other word-manipulation exercises, and have a wide knowledge of music. Good verbal and auditory memory is recognized as a contributing factor to success in careers involving languages, creative writing, performance, legal and other persuasive argument, and music or sound.

Improving your verbal and auditory abilities will help you to take in and process verbal and heard information more efficiently. You are less likely to be stuck for words and more likely to enjoy books, poetry, radio, lectures, speeches and concerts.

The verbal and auditory tests in this book are designed to exercise your verbal and auditory memory. They are not given under controlled conditions, nor have they been subjected to rigorous standardization and normalization, so they cannot provide definitive results. The score you achieve is merely meant to be an indicator of how you might perform in a professional and scientifically controlled test of verbal and auditory memory ability. In short, the results should only be interpreted as a broad estimate of this ability.

At the end of each test there are hints on how to improve your performance.

6.1 Word manipulation

This test measures your ability to manipulate words and meanings in short-term (working) memory. It also draws upon your (long-term) knowledge of English language.

You have five minutes to complete the test. Do not use reference material such as a dictionary, encyclopedia or thesaurus, and do not write anything down except the answers.

1 If the word BITE is written under the word TOOL and the word MIME is written under the word BITE and the word POPE is written under the word MIME, is the word TIME formed diagonally?

2 In a language called ZOCAROOTOO, 'ZOC ZUC ZAT' means 'We are cold', 'ZUM ZOC ZUD' means 'Trees are beautiful', 'ZUD ZOP ZAT' means 'We love trees'. Deduce how you would say 'We are beautiful' in ZOCAROOTOO from the clues above. The word order is unimportant.

3 Do the consonants in the word CALMING appear in alphabetical order?

4 In the English alphabet, how many letters are there between the letters F and T?

5 If you remove nine letters from the word INSTANTANEOUS, can the word SUIT be formed?

(test continues over the page)

6 If all Mudflats are Koots and most Mudflats are Jerries, the statement that many Koots are Jerries is:

    A. True   B. False

    C. Indeterminable

7 Which of the following words is closest in meaning to 'hindrance':

    A. Ban   B. Inconvenience

    C. Failure   D. Impediment

8 Which of the following words is closest in meaning to 'worship':

    A. Dutifulness   B. Enchantment

    C. Devotion   D. Submissiveness

Answers

7: D; 8: C

1: Yes; 2: ZAT ZOC ZUM; 3: No; 4: 13; 5: Yes; 6: A;

How did you do?

Number of correct answers (out of 8):

0–2	3–6	More than 6
→ Below average	→ Average	→ Above average

How to improve your results

To hold words in working memory for longer it helps to repeat them to yourself while 'listening' to the sounds they make. For question 1, try visualizing the words one above the other. For question 2, use associations to add meaning to the strange words, for example, once you have deduced that 'ZUM' means 'beautiful', you will hold this in mind for longer if you associate 'ZUM' with rhyming word 'mum' ('mum is beautiful') – see the link-word method on pages 122–3. Crosswords and other word puzzles will exercise your ability to manipulate words. Reading widely will help to extend your vocabulary.

6.2 Word lists

This is a test of your verbal memory span – how many words you can hold in conscious (working) memory at any one time.

On the opposite page there are three lists, each progressively more difficult. Starting with list 1, allow yourself sixty seconds to read through the items, then cover up the list and try to recall as many items as possible – write them down on a piece of paper in any order. Repeat with lists 2 and 3.

List 1

1 Grape
2 Lobster
3 Tail
4 Apple
5 Broccoli
6 Hand
7 Horse
8 Mountain
9 Graphic design
10 Buddhism
11 Magpie
12 Rogue
13 Golden goose
14 Synagogue
15 Valley
16 Motor racing

List 2

1 Soup
2 Resin
3 Oboe
4 Golf
5 Loaf
6 Lizard
7 Cowboy
8 Beetle
9 Tennis
10 Inspiration
11 Blue
12 Cricket
13 Soyabean
14 Cooker
15 Carnival
16 Golden

List 3

1 Cocaine
2 Analogy
3 Provincial
4 Newsworthy
5 Buckwheat
6 Crib
7 Multiple
8 Pacemaker
9 Niche
10 Pupil
11 Puppet
12 Statistics
13 Turmoil
14 Asset
15 Gull
16 Myth

How did you do?

Number of words recalled in each list (out of 16):

0–3	4–9	*More than 9*
→ Below average	→ Average	→ Above average

Note: Most people will not be able to remember the whole list, especially list 3, which contains more abstract terms and less familiar vocabulary. The first and last words of each list are usually relatively easy to remember; the middle words are much more difficult (Baddeley, 2004). Concrete objects are easier to remember than abstract concepts, especially those that can be visualized using striking images. Familiar words are easier than rare ones – what is familiar to you will depend upon your own particular interests and knowledge. Lists containing words that can be grouped into categories are easier than lists that are made up of unrelated items.

How to improve your performance

Visualize the objects the words represent as you read them (visualization is explained on page 110). Notice the categories the words fall into, for example, grape, lobster, apple and broccoli are all edible so group them together. Grouping items into meaningful categories helps memory and is explained on page 109. Alternatively, use the words to form a 'story', whch you can relate back to recall them. This mnemonic technique and others to remember lists are explained on pages 115–20.

6.3 Relating a heard story

This tests your ability to understand and store information presented orally and to retrieve it accurately from memory.

Ask someone to read aloud the following story, at a slow pace. Listen carefully and when they have finished write down the story in as much detail as you can. You should complete the test within ten minutes.

The legend of the brave knight, Peter Loschy...
Roger Dodsworth, the antiquarian, tells us a story he heard in 1610, which has now become part of local folklore.

There was once a valiant warrior named Peter Loschy, living in the region of the north of England, who became known throughout all the land for a great deed that he did for the locality. A fierce dragon had taken a heavy toll on the countryside, killing animals and travellers that happened to pass too close to his lair in Loschy Wood, in the manor of East Newton. Knowing the wicked deeds the dragon had done, the local people stayed in their homes at night and never went to the wood in which the dragon resided. All except Peter Loschy, who, dismayed by the restriction the dragon had placed upon their lives, one day set out to Loschy Wood, his armour strengthened by many razor blades, with the intention of destroying the fierce creature once and for all. He took with him his faithful dog. On entering the wood, a powerful dragon with luminous scales and smoke-filled nostrils confronted the brave knight. The battle that ensued was arduous and long, but Peter, wielding his heavy iron sword, managed to slice off pieces of the dragon bit by bit. Each bloody morsel was triumphantly removed by his faithful dog and carried to the opposite hillside, to Nunnington churchyard, where the pieces were buried below the root of a cedar tree. At length the fatal blow was given, and the remaining item, the head, was carried away by the dog. The satisfied dog, whose tongue was now saturated with the dragon's poison, then licked its master's face in gratification. Both master and dog died shortly afterwards from poisoning.

How did you do?
Check your version with the original and assess your performance:

You fail to recall the main events of the story.
➜ Below average

Your story departs from the original in two or three places, and some of the details are missing, but generally it follows the original.
➜ Average

The details are recalled accurately and the story follows the original.
➜ Above average

Note: The story you remember is usually shorter, more coherent, and more biased towards your own views (Bartlett, 1932). This tends to show up particularly with material that does not satisfy expectations – you adapt the story to fit in with your own world view. Bartlett found that it is usual for recall to be influenced by your attitude to the piece. This determines, for example, which side you take in a reported quarrel, and the details you remember; in other words, it is difficult to be truly objective in reporting back the story. The resulting 'distortion' in perception and memory is a genuine cause for concern in the real-world practice of eyewitness testimony.

How to improve your performance

See pages 100–2 for advice on improving concentration. As you listen to the story, visualize the events going on, in all their colourful detail (see page 110 for more on visualization). Notice the structure of the piece: how it begins, the main events, how it ends. Fix this in your mind before you write anything down: it will act as a prompt for recalling the details you visualized during the reading. Mnemonic techniques for remembering the main features of a story and the order in which they occur are given on pages 115–18 (the method of loci and the narrative story method).

End of tests

6

FINAL ASSESSMENT

How to make the final assessment

You have reached the final assessment in this book. Use it to check if your memory has improved in the following areas:

Test 1: Social/adaptive memory (names and faces, birthdays and anniversaries, appointments)

Test 2: Visual–spatial memory (scene, abstract drawing, mental rotation, spatial orientation)

Test 3: Working memory (playing cards, word pairs, reading)

Test 4: Factual memory (facts, definitions)

Test 5: Numerical memory (mental calculation, telephone numbers)

Test 6: Verbal and auditory memory (word manipulation, word lists)

These tests are the most challenging in the book, but if you have followed the advice in chapters four and five, and practised memory-improving techniques, your scores should be at least as good as those for the preliminary assessment test. Ideally, you should achieve a marked improvement in performance.

As for previous tests, note that memory performance depends on individual interests and experiences and there is no single objective scale against which to measure the effectiveness of your memory. The tests cannot provide definitive results but will give an indication of your memory's efficiency and development.

Begin final assessment

Test 1: Social/adaptive memory
1.1 Names and faces
Take two minutes to memorize the names and faces of the people illustrated on the page opposite, then turn the page.

Serge Halimi

Hillary Bayh

Carlos Vidal

Daniela Villani

Alexander Nickell

Archie Hochschild

Felix Logan

Inga Waliszewski

Akira Nikitenko

Tony Atela

Write down the name of each person.

- - - - - - - - - - - - - - - -

- - - - - - - - - - - - - - - -

How did you do?

Number of faces and names recalled (out of 10):

0–2	*3–6*	*More than 6*
→ Below average	→ Average	→ Above average

1.2 Birthdays and anniversaries

Write down all the birthdays and anniversaries you can remember in sixty seconds. Use a separate sheet of paper if necessary.

Birthdays

Name   Date

-----------------------------   -----------------------------

-----------------------------   -----------------------------

-----------------------------   -----------------------------

-----------------------------   -----------------------------

-----------------------------   -----------------------------

-----------------------------   -----------------------------

-----------------------------   -----------------------------

-----------------------------   -----------------------------

-----------------------------   -----------------------------

-----------------------------   -----------------------------

-----------------------------   -----------------------------

-----------------------------   -----------------------------

-----------------------------   -----------------------------

-----------------------------   -----------------------------

Anniversaries

Name   Date

---------------------------   ---------------------------
---------------------------   ---------------------------
---------------------------   ---------------------------
---------------------------   ---------------------------
---------------------------   ---------------------------
---------------------------   ---------------------------
---------------------------   ---------------------------
---------------------------   ---------------------------
---------------------------   ---------------------------
---------------------------   ---------------------------
---------------------------   ---------------------------
---------------------------   ---------------------------
---------------------------   ---------------------------
---------------------------   ---------------------------

How did you do?

Number of dates recalled:

0–2	*3–6*	*More than 6*
→ Below average	→ Average	→ Above average

1.3 Appointments

Look at the following page from a diary showing the planned events of the coming week. Take three minutes to memorize the information, then turn the page.

MARCH

6   **Monday**
10.30 am   *Meet Alexei at 52 Sarandon Street*
2 pm   *Sales meeting*
7 pm   *French class*

---

7   **Tuesday**
9 am   *Interviews for new Stage Manager*
2 pm   *Finance meeting*
8 pm   *Phone Lidia*

---

8   **Wednesday**
8.30 am   *Check in for flight to Moscow*
4.30 pm   *Meet Ivan Dashkov at the Petrovsky Theatre*
7 pm   *Dinner with Lidia and Johann*

---

9   **Thursday**
10.15 am   *Check in for flight to St Petersburg*
12 noon   *Lunch meeting with Laurence, Kirov Theatre*
6 pm   *Drinks, Konyushennaya Street*

---

10   **Friday**
6 am   *Check in for flight home*

---

11   **Saturday**
          Petra's birthday

---

12   **Sunday**

Try and recall the diary entries below:

Monday

Tuesday

Wednesday

Thursday

Friday

Saturday

Sunday

How did you do?

Number of diary entries recalled (out of 14):

| *0–2* | *3–7* | *More than* 7 |
| ➜ Below average | ➜ Average | ➜ Above average |

Test 2: Visual–spatial memory
2.1 Scene

Study the picture below for two minutes. Then turn the page and answer the questions.

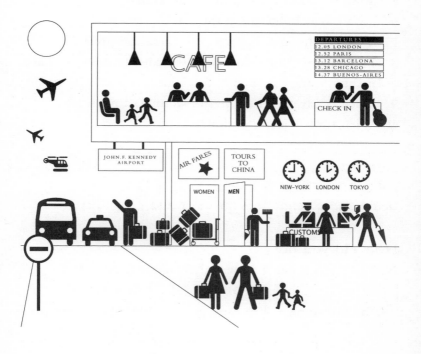

1 How many cases does the man waiting for the taxi have?
2 What time is it in Tokyo?
3 When is the next departure for Barcelona?
4 What is the man checking in at the check-in desk?
5 Who is coming out of the men's toilets?
6 How many lights are in the café?
7 When is the next departure for Buenos Aires?
8 How many cases does the woman at customs have, including the case being searched?
9 What is advertised above the women's toilets?
10 What time is it in London?

Answers

1: 6; 2: 11 pm; 3: 13.12; 4: A guitar; 5: A cleaner;
6: 4; 7: 14.37; 8: 3; 9: Air fares; 10: 2 pm

How did you do?

Number of questions answered correctly (out of 10):

| *0–2* | *3–6* | *More than 6* |
| → Below average | → Average | → Above average |

2.2 Abstract drawing

Study the abstract drawing for two minutes. Draw it on a piece of paper if it helps to lodge it in memory. Then turn over the page and recreate the drawing from memory.

Recreate the drawing from memory here:

How did you do?

Compare your drawing with the original and check the following:

	Yes	No
1 Did you remember the main structure of the figure (the overall shape and main intersecting lines)?		
2 Did you remember more than 50% of the incidental (non-structural) elements?		
3 Did you remember less than 50% of the incidental (non-structural) elements?		

You answered 'no' to questions 1 and 2, and 'yes' to question 3.
→ Below average

You answered 'yes' to question 1 and show a good memory for the structure and organization of visual information. You probably interpreted the structure in terms of an object it reminded you of, which helped you to recall the overall shape. You remembered some of the other details but perhaps not as much as 50%.
→ Average

You answered 'yes' to questions 1 and 2.
→ Above average

2.3 Mental rotation

Look closely at the cube cluster A. Then mentally rotate each cube cluster B–E and decide which ones if any are the same as the cube cluster A. There is a time limit of three minutes.

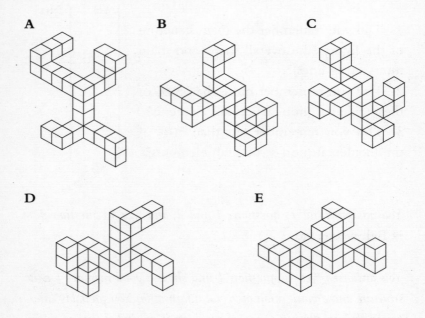

A　　　　　　　B　　　　　　　C

D　　　　　　　E

Answer

ʻⱯ ɹǝʇsnʃɔ ǝqnɔ ǝɥʇ sɐ ǝɯɐs ǝɥʇ ǝɹɐ ᗡ puɐ ᗺ sǝqnƆ

How did you do?

Number of matching cube clusters identified (out of 2):

Zero	One	Two
→ Below average	→ Average	→ Above average

2.4 Spatial orientation

'A' marks your position on the map below. Study the map for two minutes, then turn the page and answer the questions.

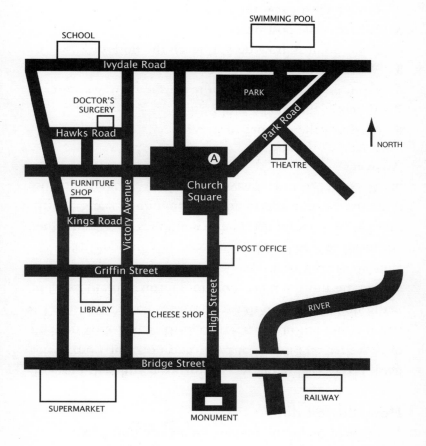

Final Assessment

Write down your answers to the following questions without looking at the map.

1 From point A, how do you reach the park?
2 On which street is the railway?
3 Where is the post office?
4 From point A, how do you reach the library?
5 Where is the swimming pool?
6 From point A, how do you reach the railway station?
7 Where is the cheese shop?
8 Where is the doctor's surgery?

Answers

1: From the church square, go east along Park Road. Turn left at the T-junction onto Ivydale Road. The park is soon after, on your left; 2: Bridge Street; 3: On the High Street; 4: From the church square, go south down the High Street and take the first turning on your right, Griffin Street. The library is on the left just after you cross over Victory Avenue; 5: Opposite the park on Ivydale Road; 6: From the church square, go south down the High Street. Turn left into Bridge Street. Continue over the bridge and the railway is on your right; 7: On Victory Avenue; 8: On Hawks Road

How did you do?

Number of questions answered correctly (out of 8):

0–2	3–6	More than 6
→ Below average	→ Average	→ Above average

Test 3: Working memory

3.1 Playing cards

You have three minutes to memorize these cards. Then turn the page and answer the question.

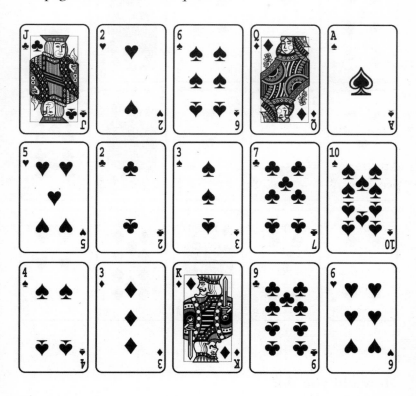

Ten of the fifteen cards on the previous page are repeated below. Which are they?

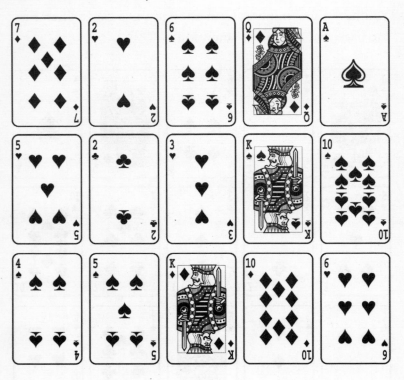

How did you do?

Number of cards recognized (out of 10):

0–2	3–7	More than 7
→ Below average	→ Average	→ Above average

3.2 Word pairs

Take sixty seconds to memorize the following pairs of words. Then turn the page.

1	Image	Nature
2	Rustle	Solid
3	Translation	Urgency
4	Earth	Imaginary
5	Mercenary	Prickle
6	Rhythm	Supersede
7	Transparent	Wince
8	Election	Liquid
9	Mosaic	Prerequisite
10	Supply	Tuning fork

Write down the paired word for each of the following:

1	Image	---------------------------------
2	Rustle	---------------------------------
3	Translation	---------------------------------
4	Earth	---------------------------------
5	Mercenary	---------------------------------
6	Rhythm	---------------------------------
7	Transparent	---------------------------------
8	Election	---------------------------------
9	Mosaic	---------------------------------
10	Supply	---------------------------------

How did you do?

Number of paired words recalled (out of 10):

| *0–5* | *6–9* | *All 10* |
| ➜ Below average | ➜ Average | ➜ Above average |

3.3 Reading memory

Read the following (abridged) extract from *The Rise and Fall of the Irish Nation* by Sir Jonah Barrington, and the introduction, which sets the context. Then turn the page and answer the questions without looking back at the text. You have six minutes to complete the whole test.

Introduction

A revolutionary movement in Ireland, inspired by the example of the American and French Revolutions, launched an uprising opposing English rule in 1798. The attack on the castle in Dublin by rebel forces from surrounding villages lacked leadership and organization. This short account begins with the loyalist forces crouching in the cattle market in Dublin town, north of the castle, awaiting the expected assault by the rebels...

Extract

All the barristers, attorneys, merchants, bankers, revenue officers, shop-keepers, students of the University, doctors, apothecaries, and members of corporations of the immense metropolis of Dublin, in red coats, with a sprinkling of parsons, all doubled up together amidst bullock stalls and sheep pens, awaiting, in profound darkness, for invisible executioners to dispatch them without mercy, was not a situation to

engender much hilarity. Scouts now and then came only to
report their ignorance; a running buzz occasionally went
round that the vedettes* were driven in; the sound of distant
musketry gave a slight but perceptible movement to men's
muscles, like a twitch of electricity; and a few faintly-heard
shots on the north side seemed to announce that the van-
guard of the Santry men was approaching. In the meantime,
no orders came from the general. It appeared, at break of day,
that both Santry and Rathfarnham rebels had adjourned
their assault to some other opportunity...

Meanwhile, the rebels had learned that the yeomanry
was ready to receive them and contented themselves with
shooting some mail coachmen, and burning some houses,
until morning dispersed them. The rebels on the south had
intended to take the castle by surprise whilst the Santry men
assailed the barracks, but their plan had been disconcerted
by Lord Roden, at the head of his dragoons (called the 'fox
hunters' because of their noble horses). His Lordship, sup-
ported by a small number of light infantry, had marched rapidly upon them, surprising the few who had collected; his
attack had completely succeeded. A few rebels were sabred,
and several more made prisoners; the main body dispersed
with little resistance. Lord Roden received a bullet on his
helmet, but was only bruised, and some of the dragoons
were wounded. The other rebels (from the county of Dublin)

---

* the mounted sentinels posted beyond the outposts of the loyalist forces

retreated to join the Kildare men. The defeated southern group marched to unite themselves with those of Wicklow. Their plan had been excellent – had they acted steadily on it, success was not improbable – but now the metropolis, at least for the time being, had no further dread of molestation.

A disgusting and horrid scene was next morning publicly exhibited, after which military executions commenced, and continued with unabating activity. Some dead bodies of insurgents, sabred the night before by Lord Roden's dragoons, were brought in a cart to Dublin, together with some prisoners tied together. The carcasses were stretched out in the castle yard, where the Viceroy then resided, in full view of the windows. There they lay on the pavement through the hot day, as trophies of the first skirmish, cut and gashed in every part, covered with clotted blood and dust – the most frightful spectacle which ever disgraced a royal residence, save the seraglio. After several hours' exposure, some appearance of life was perceived in one of the mutilated carcasses. The man had been stabbed and gashed in various parts. His body was removed into the guardroom, and attempts were made to restore animation. The efforts succeeded; he entirely recovered, and was pardoned by Lord Camden. He was an extraordinarily fine young man, above six feet high, the son of a Mr Keogh, an opulent landholder of Rathfarnham. He did not, however, change his principles, and was ultimately sent out of the country.

1 In which year was the uprising launched?

2 Who was crouching in the cattle market awaiting the rebels?

3 What had the rebels planned to do before their plan was frustrated?

4 What was the name of Lord Roden's dragoons?

5 What injuries did Lord Roden receive, if any?

6 What was the horrid scene the next morning?

7 Who was the rebel that recovered from his wounds?

8 What happened to him?

Answers

1: 1798; **2:** The loyalist forces: barristers, attorneys, merchants, bankers, revenue officers, shop-keepers, university students, doctors, apothecaries, members of Dublin's corporations, and several parsons; **3:** Rebels on the south were to take the castle by surprise while the Santry rebels attacked the barracks; **4:** The 'fox hunters'; **5:** Bruising caused by a bullet to the helmet; **6:** Dead bodies of rebels displayed in the castle yard; executions of rebels; **7:** The son of a Mr Keogh, an opulent landholder of Rathfarnham; **8:** He did not change his principles and was later sent out of the country

How did you do?

Number of questions answered correctly (out of 8):

0–2	3–5	More than 5
→ Below average	→ Average	→ Above average

Test 4: Factual memory
4.1 Recall of facts

Write down the answers to the following questions (the answers are on the following page). You have sixty seconds to complete the test.

1 When was the Bay of Pigs Invasion?
2 When did the Vietnam War end?
3 What is the capital of Kenya?
4 What is the capital of Norway?
5 Who wrote the songs 'I've Been Loving You Too Long', 'Try a Little Tenderness', 'Mr Pitiful', 'Satisfaction', '(Sittin' On The) Dock of the Bay', and 'Respect'?
6 Who took the lead male role in the film *It's a Wonderful Life* (1946)?
7 Who painted *The Scream* (1895)?
8 What year did the United States enter World War II?
9 What year was the Wall Street Crash?
10 Which president of the United States came after John F. Kennedy in 1963?

Answers

1: 1961; **2:** 1975; **3:** Nairobi; **4:** Oslo; **5:** Otis Redding;
6: James Stewart; **7:** Edvard Munch; **8:** 1941; **9:** 1929;
10: Lyndon B. Johnson

How did you do?

Number of facts recalled (out of 10):

0–2	*3–6*	*More than 6*
➜ Below average	➜ Average	➜ Above average

Now look up ten new facts you do not already know and learn them. Use the spaces below to record a question that will test your knowledge of each fact. Test yourself in a week's time.

1 ---

2 ---

3 ---

4 ---

5 ---

6 ---

7 ---

8 ---

9 ---

10 --

4.2 Definitions

Read the definitions and produce the target words as quickly as possible (the answers are on the following page). You
have sixty seconds to complete the test.

Definition	Target word
1 The region or environment where a plant or animal normally grows or lives.	------------------
2 To regulate more than one thing so as to agree in time or rate of speed.	------------------
3 An ancient Greek, Roman or Egyptian coffin or tomb, inscribed and elaborately ornamented.	------------------
4 A great and sudden disaster, calamity or misfortune.	------------------
5 Daring and fearless; showing a readiness to take risks.	------------------
6 A dark shape or figure seen against a light background.	------------------
7 The science dealing with the physical nature and history of the earth.	------------------
8 A partial or total obscuring of one celestial body by another.	------------------
9 Something that can live both on land and in water.	------------------
10 Favouring no one side more than another.	------------------

Answers
1: Habitat; **2:** Synchronize; **3:** Sarcophagus; **4:** Catastrophe;
5: Bold; **6:** Silhouette; **7:** Geology; **8:** Eclipse;
9: Amphibian; **10:** Impartial

How did you do?
Number of correct target words (out of 10):

0–2	*3–7*	*More than 7*
→ Below average	→ Average	→ Above average

Test 5: Numerical memory
5.1 Mental calculation

Follow the route below, making the required calculations along the way. Do not write anything down. Allow yourself four minutes to complete the test.

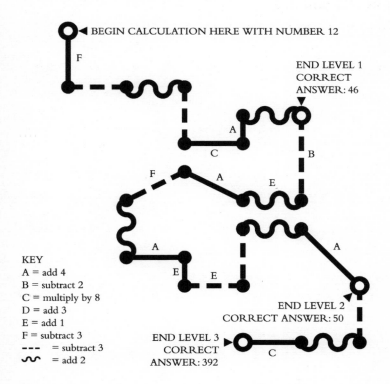

BEGIN CALCULATION HERE WITH NUMBER 12

END LEVEL 1
CORRECT
ANSWER: 46

END LEVEL 2
CORRECT ANSWER: 50

END LEVEL 3
CORRECT
ANSWER: 392

KEY
A = add 4
B = subtract 2
C = multiply by 8
D = add 3
E = add 1
F = subtract 3
--- = subtract 3
∿ = add 2

How did you do?

Calculation error during level 1	*Calculation error during level 2*	*Calculation correct up to level 3*
→ Below average	→ Average	→ Above average

5.2 Telephone numbers

Write down all the telephone numbers you can remember in sixty seconds.

Name   **Number**

-------------------------   -------------------------
-------------------------   -------------------------
-------------------------   -------------------------
-------------------------   -------------------------
-------------------------   -------------------------
-------------------------   -------------------------
-------------------------   -------------------------
-------------------------   -------------------------
-------------------------   -------------------------
-------------------------   -------------------------
-------------------------   -------------------------
-------------------------   -------------------------

Now record two useful telephone numbers you would like to learn, for example, the number of a friend, your bank, your doctor's surgery, the garage or the school. You have sixty seconds to memorize the numbers, then turn the page.

Name   **Number**

-------------------------   -------------------------
-------------------------   -------------------------

Wait one hour before writing down the numbers you just
memorized. Keep testing yourself regularly to lodge them in
long-term memory.

Name   **Number**

-------------------------   -------------------------

-------------------------   -------------------------

How did you do?

Recall of telephone numbers learnt in the past:

| *0–2* | *3–6* | *More than 6* |
| → Below average | → Average | → Above average |

Recall of telephone numbers newly memorized (out of 2):

| *None* | *1* | *2* |
| → Below average | → Average | → Above average |

Test 6: Verbal and auditory memory
6.1 Word manipulation

You have five minutes to answer the questions. Do not use reference material such as a dictionary, encyclopedia or thesaurus, and do not write anything down except the answers.

1 If the word MEET is written under the word MAUL and the word SENT is written under the word MEET and the word POLE is written under the word SENT, is the word PEEL formed diagonally from bottom left-hand corner to top-right?

2 In a language called MATEY, 'MAT MEL MOT' means 'She loves Tom', 'MEL MOO MIN' means 'She is here', 'MIN MOT MUT' means 'Tom is home'. Deduce how you would say 'She is home' in MATEY from the clues above. The word order is unimportant.

3 Do the consonants in the word COMPUTER appear in alphabetical order?

4 In the English alphabet, how many consonants are there between the letters B and T?

5 If you remove six letters from the word XENOPHOBIA, can the word 'BONE' be formed?

6 If all Vics are Jubs and many Vics are Zubs, the statement that few Jubs are Zubs is:
   A. True   B. False
   C. Indeterminable

(test continues over the page)

7 Which of the following words is closest in meaning to 'adversity':

   A. Catastrophe   B. Bad luck

   C. Mishap   D. Wretchedness

8 Which of the following words is closest in meaning to 'indifference':

   A. Unconcern   B. Disinclination

   C. Reluctance   D. Distaste

Answers

6: B; 7: D; 8: A

1: Yes; 2: MEL MIN MUT; 3: No; 4: 14; 5: Yes;

How did you do?

Number of correct answers (out of 8):

0–2	3–6	More than 6
→ Below average	→ Average	→ Above average

6.2 Word lists

Starting with list 1, allow yourself sixty seconds to read through the items, then cover up the list and try to recall as many items as you can — write them down on a piece of paper. Repeat with lists 2 and 3.

List 1	List 2	List 3
1 Synaesthesia	1 Pardon	1 Imply
2 Recognize	2 Multiply	2 Output
3 Hammer	3 Interrupt	3 Status
4 Card	4 Manual	4 Symmetry
5 Lasagne	5 Pastel	5 View
6 Stove	6 Severe	6 Wisdom
7 Tulip	7 Turnpike	7 Slogan
8 Physics	8 Fragile	8 Pocket
9 Onion	9 Combine	9 Plunge
10 Daughter	10 Grasp	10 Manners
11 Bass	11 Productive	11 Satellite
12 Conscious	12 Tenancy	12 Genuine
13 Kiosk	13 Symbiosis	13 Dose
14 Conker	14 Petition	14 Cylinder
15 Nitric acid	15 Load	15 Assertive
16 Secular	16 Industrial	16 Almond

How did you do?

Number of words recalled in each list (out of 16):

0–3	4–9	*More than 9*
→ Below average	→ Average	→ Above average

End of final assessment

Have you improved your memory?

Now that you have completed the final assessment, compare your scores with the preliminary assessment and check that you have achieved your objectives for memory improvement. Make a note of the most useful techniques you used and how you applied them. Refer to your notes later on to make sure you are still using and practising the techniques.

Do not stop with these tests. Keep recalling and checking the information you have learnt. Over-learning material ensures that your memories are durable and can help to boost your confidence.

POSTSCRIPT

Memory ability is not simply a case of having a good or bad memory. There are multiple areas of memory functioning and most people are good in some areas and not others. This may partly be determined by how we are biologically wired, but strengths and weaknesses also undoubtedly reflect how often we practise each function, which in turn reflects our interests, experience and career choice: an architect will exercise visual–spatial memory regularly and under critical conditions; a journalist will rely heavily on verbal and audi-tory memory; a teacher may develop a reliable memory for facts. Those who recognize the potential benefits to social and business life of possessing a good memory across a range of functions may well seek to enhance memory perform-ance in all areas regardless of vocation and interests.

With practice, most memory problems can be resolved. Many are due to poor attention and concentration. Inefficient encoding and retrieval of information are also common causes of memory failure. Recognizing how mem-ory fails is an important step towards realizing more of our amazing potential to remember things.

REFERENCES AND FURTHER READING

Ad Herennium (c. 80 BC), English translation (1954), Harry Caplan, Harvard University Press, Cambridge, MA

Atkinson, R.C. & Shiffrin, R.M. (1968), 'Human memory: A proposed system and its control processes', in K.W. Spence (ed.), *The Psychology of Learning & Motivation: Advances in Research and Theory*, Vol 2, New York: Academic Press, 89–195

Atkinson, R.C. & Shiffrin, R.M. (1971), 'The control of short-term memory', *Scientific American*, 224, 82–90

Baddeley, Alan (2004), *Your Memory, A User's Guide*, Carlton Books

Baddeley, A.D., Emslie, H. & Nimmo-Smith, I. (1995), 'The Doors and People Test', Thames Valley Test Company

Baddeley, A.D. & Hitch, G. (1974), 'Working memory' in G.H. Bower (ed.) *Recent Advances in Learning and Motivation*, Vol 8, New York: Academic Press

Baltes, P.G. & Kliegl, R. (1992), 'Further testing of limits of cognitive plasticity: Negative age differences in a mnemonic skill are robust', *Developmental Psychology*, 28, 121–5

Baron, R.A. (1989), *Psychology: The Essential Science*, London: Allyn & Bacon

Barrington, Sir Jonah (1833), *The Rise and Fall of the Irish Nation*, London

Bartlett, F. (1932), *Remembering*, Cambridge University Press

Belezza, F.S. (1981), 'Mnemonic devices: Classification, characteristics and criteria', *Review of Educational Research*, 51, 247–75

Bousfield, W.A. (1953), 'The occurrence of clustering in the recall of randomly arranged associates', *Journal of General Psychology*, 49, 229–40

Bower, G.H. (1972), 'Mental imagery and associative learning', in L. Gregg (ed.), *Cognition in Learning and Memory*, New York: Wiley

Bower, G.H. & Clark, M.C. (1969), 'Narrative stories as mediators for serial learning', *Psychonomic Science*, 14, 181–2

Bower, G.H. & Hilgard, E.R. (1981), *Theories of Learning*, Englewood Cliffs, NJ: Prentice Hall

Butterworth, Brian (1999), *The Mathematical Brain*, Macmillan

Cicero, *De oratore* (55 BC), translation (1942), E.W. Sutton & H. Rackham Cambridge: Harvard University Press

Cohen, G. (1990), 'Memory', in I. Roth (ed.) *Introduction to Psychology*, Vol 2, Milton Keynes: Open University Press

Collins, A.M. & Quillian, M.R. (1969), 'Retrieval time from semantic memory', *Journal of Verbal Learning and Verbal Behavior*, 8, 240–8

Collins, A.M. & Quillian, M.R. (1972), 'How to make a language user', in E. Tulving & W. Donaldson (eds.) *Organization of Memory*, New York: Academic Press

Craik, F.I.M. & Lockhart, R.S. (1972), 'Levels of processing: A framework for memory research', *Journal of Verbal Learning and Verbal Behavior*, 11, 671–84

Dickens, C. (1853), *Bleak House*, London

Ebbinghaus, H. (1885), 'Über das Gedachtnis', Leipzig: Duncker, translated in 1913 and 1964 as *Memory*

Finkel, Robert (1992), *Memory Booster*, Judy Piatkus

Frieman, Jerome, L. (2002), *Learning and Adaptive Behavior*, Florence, KY: Wadsworth Publishing

Gross, R. and McIlveen, R. (1999), *Aspects of Psychology: Memory*, Hodder & Stoughton

Gruneberg, Michael M. (1992), 'The Practical Application of Memory Aids', in M.M. Gruneberg, M.M. & Morris, P. (eds.), *Aspects of Memory, Vol 1: The Practical Aspects*, London: Routledge

Haselbauer, Nathan (2009), *How Good Is Your IQ?*, Constable & Robinson

Higbee, Kenneth L. (2001), *Your Memory: How It Works & How to Improve It*, 2nd edition, Marlowe & Company

Howarth, C.I. & Gillham, W.E.C. (eds.) (1981), *The Structure of Psychology*, George Allen & Unwin

James, W. (1890), *The Principles of Psychology*, New York: Henry Holt

Kemper, S. (1990), 'Adults' diaries: Changes made to written narratives across the life-span', *Discourse Processes*, 13

Landauer, T.K. & Bjork, R.A. (1978), 'Optimum rehearsal patterns and name learning', in M.M. Gruneberg, P.E.

Morris and R.N. Sykes (eds.), *Practical Aspects of Memory*, London: Academic Press, 625–32

Linton, M. (1978), 'Real world memory after six years: An in vivo study of very long-term memory', in M.M. Gruneberg, P.E. Morris and R.N. Sykes (eds.), *Practical Aspects of Memory*, London: Academic Press, 69–76

Luria, A.R. (1968), *The Mind of a Mnemonist*, translated from the Russian by Lynn Solotaroff, Basic Books, Inc

Mason, D.J. & Kohn, M.L. (2001), *The Memory Workbook*, New Harbinger Publications

McCarty, D.L. (1980), 'Investigation of a visual imagery mnemonic device for acquiring face-name associations', *Journal of Experimental Psychology: Human Learning and Memory*, 6, 145–55

Mérimée, Prosper (1833), *Mosaïque*

Miller, G.A. (1956), 'The magical number seven, plus or minus two: Some limits on our capacity for processing information', *Psychological Review*, 63, 81–97

Quintilian (first century AD), *Institutio oratorio*, English translation (1921–2), Harold Edgeworth Butler

Rabbitt, P.M.A. (1989), 'Inner-city decay? Age changes in structure and process in recall of familiar topographical information', in L. Poon, D. Rubin & B.A. Wilson (eds.), *Everyday Cognition in Adult and Later Life*, Cambridge University Press

Robertson-Tchabo, E.A. (1980), 'Cognitive-skill training for the elderly: Why should 'old dogs' acquire new tricks?', in *New Directions in Memory and Aging: Proceedings of the George A. Talland Memorial Conference*, L. Poon, J.L. Fozard, L.S. Cermak, D. Arenberg & L.W. Thompson (eds.), Hillsdale, NJ: Erlbaum

Rose, Steven (1992), *The Making of Memory*, Bantam Books

Tulving, E. (1966), 'Subjective organization and effects of repetition in multi-trial free-recall learning', *Journal of Verbal Learning and Verbal Behavior*, 5, 193–7

Tulving, E. & Osler, S. (1968), 'Effectiveness of retrieval cues in memory for words', *Journal of Experimental Psychology*, 77, 593–601

West, R.L. & T.H. Crook (1992), 'Video training of imagery for mature adults', *Applied Cognitive Psychology*, 6, 307–20

Williams, M. & Burden, R. (1997), *Psychology for Language Teachers*, Cambridge University Press

Yates, Frances, A. (1992), *The Art of Memory*, Pimlico

GLOSSARY

Alzheimer's disease

A progressive, irreversible disease involving the degeneration of cognitive functions (including memory, perception and judgment), leading to severe mental impairment.

Amnesia

A condition involving loss of memory of events within a specific period of time.

Association

A method of encoding information that involves linking together new information with things we already know. The association acts as a trigger for the retrieval of the new information when we want to recall it from memory.

Attention

The act of focusing one's mind closely on something, or noticing or observing things.

Chunking

A technique of grouping together pieces of information to make it more meaningful, and therefore memorable. For example, grouping together the digits of a number into twos and threes, representing international and local codes, or the grouping together of letters to form words in normal language formation.

Computer model of memory

This models memory functioning on the functioning of a computer. Information is taken in and processed (encoded), stored in memory and retrieved from memory.

Concentration

Sustained attention on something over a period of time.

Cortex

The outer layer of the brain.

Depth of processing

A model of memory introduced by Craik and Lockhart (1972). It proposes that efficient memory storage is dependent on how well an item of information is encoded: deeper processing, and more effective memory, results from encoding in a meaningful way, using sensory information and associations with personal knowledge and experience.

Encoding

The process of acquiring new memories, which involves first registering the information and then processing it into a form that allows it to be stored in memory.

Episodic memory
Storage of information about one's life history, including what you did last week, where you were born, where you first learnt something, etc.

External memory strategies
Methods for remembering things that involve writing things down, making lists, using a diary and other aids such as an alarm clock, tape recorder, calendar, wall chart, etc.

Factual memory
The ability to remember facts, including knowledge about the world (historical, geographical, scientific and cultural facts) and sensory knowledge (such as knowing the smell of the sea or the taste of butter).

Hippocampus
A part of the brain that lies underneath the temporal lobe and is known to be important in memory.

Internal memory strategies
Methods for remembering things that rely on a learnt strategy rather than relying on writing things down.

Learning
The ability to acquire knowledge and skills, and to change behaviour and perceptions through experience in order to adapt to one's environment. It is closely linked to memory.

Long-term memory store

This is what most people refer to as memory. It is the memory store where we hold virtually permanent information that we commit to memory in order to retrieve it at a later time.

Memory

The process of taking in information from the environment through the senses, organizing and storing this information, and recalling the information at a later time.

Mnemonics

Specific systems or techniques for improving memory functioning.

Numerical memory

The ability to remember information presented in numerical form rather than in words or pictures.

Perception

The mental process of interpreting information taken in by the senses.

Procedural memory

The ability to remember how to do things, like riding a bicycle or driving a car, that once learnt brings about automatic and conditioned behaviour.

Prospective memory

The ability to remember plans for the future, from keeping an appointment to our plans for life.

Retrieval

The process of getting memories out of storage and into our conscious minds. There are two types of retrieval: recall and recognition. Recall is remembering what happened last week or remembering a fact to answer an exam question. Recognition is remembering which road leads home or identifying the correct answer in a multiple-choice test.

Sensory memory store

A store that receives information from the environment – through vision, hearing, touch, taste and feel. The information stays in our sensory memory store for a fraction of a second before it is either forgotten or transferred to short-term memory.

Semantic memory

The ability to remember information about the world, including facts (such as the capital of Chile) and sensory knowledge (such as knowing the taste of butter).

Short–term memory store

The memory store that holds information for only a short period between taking it in via sensory filters and storing it in long-term memory. The working memory model (Baddeley & Hitch, 1974) is a popular theory of short-term memory.

Social/adaptive memory

The ability to remember information relating to social settings, including the knowledge that allows us to function effectively and meet social or community expectations.

Storage

The process of holding onto memories, sometimes likened to filing. How information is stored affects how efficiently it is recalled. Information stored in an organized way and attached to meaningful information already in store is easier to remember.

Verbal and auditory memory

The ability to remember information presented verbally (using words), especially information that we hear rather than see.

Visualization

A method helpful in memory that involves forming a mental image of something not currently present to the sight.

Visual–spatial memory

The ability to remember information perceived visually, including spatial relations between objects and in relation to oneself.

Working memory store/model

Sometimes called 'short-term', 'conscious' or 'active' memory, this is a temporary store of limited capacity containing everything we are conscious of, and working on, at the current moment in time. Working memory holds information while we are using it to understand things or while it is being processed for long-term memory storage.

INDEX

Three ways to order *Right Way* books:

(1) Visit www.constablerobinson.com and order through our website.

(2) Telephone the TBS order line on 01206 255 800.
Order lines are open Monday – Friday, 8:30am – 5:30pm.

(3) Use this order form and send a cheque made payable to **TBS Ltd** or charge my   [ ] Visa   [ ] Mastercard   [ ] Maestro (issue no   )

Card number: _____

Expiry date: _____   Last three digits on back of card: _____

Signature: _____

(your signature is essential when paying by credit or debit card)

No. of copies	Title	Price	Total
	How Good is Your IQ?	£5.99	
	For P&P add £2.75 for the first book, 60p for each additional book		
	Grand Total		£

Name: _____
Address: _____
_____   Postcode: _____

Daytime Tel. No./Email _____
(in case of query)

Please return forms to Cash Sales/Direct Mail Dept., The Book Service, Colchester Road, Frating Green, Colchester CO7 7DW.

Enquiries to readers@constablerobinson.com.

Constable and Robinson Ltd (directly or via its agents) may mail, email or phone you about promotions or products.

[ ] Tick box if you do not want these from us [ ] or our subsidiaries.

www.right-way.co.uk
www.constablerobinson.com